Nine Mile Canyon

D1608313

NINE MILE CANYON

The
Archaeological
History
of an
American
Treasure

JERRY D. SPANGLER

THE UNIVERSITY OF UTAH PRESS
Salt Lake City

Publication of this book made possible in part
by a generous grant from the Bill Barrett Corporation.

The Defiance House Man colophon is a registered trademark of
the University of Utah Press. It is based on a four-foot-tall Ancient
Puebloan pictograph (late PIII) near Glen Canyon, Utah.

17 16 15 14 13   1 2 3 4 5

LIBRARY OF CONGRESS CATALOGING-IN-PUBLICATION DATA

Spangler, Jerry D.
  Nine mile canyon : the archaeological history of an
American treasure / Jerry D. Spangler.
      p. cm.
  Includes bibliographical references and index.
  ISBN 978-1-60781-226-5 (pbk. : alk. paper)
  ISBN 978-1-60781-228-9 (ebook)
  1. Indians of North America—Utah—Nine Mile Canyon—Antiquities.
  2. Petroglyphs—Utah—Nine Mile Canyon. 3. Rock paintings—Utah—
Nine Mile Canyon. 4. Nine Mile Canyon (Utah)—Antiquities. I. Title.
  E78.U55S63 2012
  709.01'1309792566—dc23
                                                          2012031967

Printed in China.

Contents

List of Maps

Acknowledgments

This book was made possible through the generous contributions of countless individuals: those who donated photographs, colleagues who offered insightful commentary along the way, and experts who shared their own unpublished research. And thank you to the many libraries and museums that opened up their archives to me. In particular, I want to thank Dr. Steven LeBlanc and the Peabody Museum staff for their invaluable assistance over the years as I have perused their collections time and again, and who then generously contributed publication rights to their photographs. And a special thanks to the talented lens-smith Ray Boren, who donated many of the Nine Mile Canyon photographs used here. And to my lovely and patient wife, Donna, my muse.

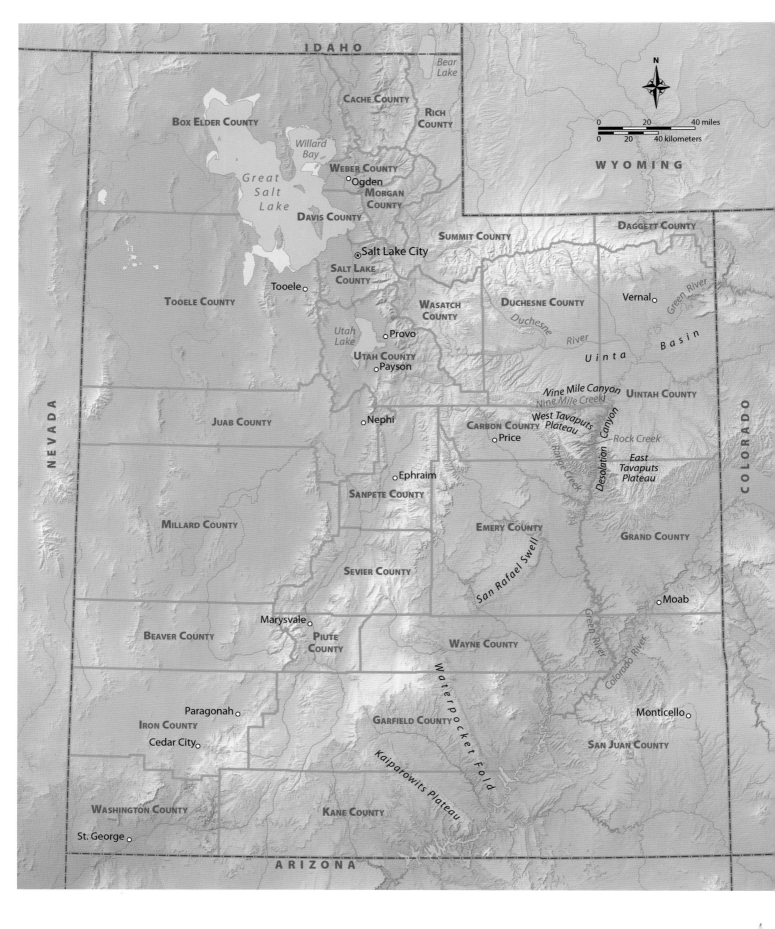

Introduction

Your appointment made today. Salary $2,100 and railroad expenses.

—George Thomas to John P. Gillin, 1935

The July 9, 1935, Western Union telegram confirming the appointment of John Phillip Gillin, "Jack" to his friends and colleagues, as "instructor" at the University of Utah's Department of Anthropology and Sociology may have seemed emotionless and succinct (Thomas 1935d). In reality, it culminated weeks of animated correspondence between Gillin and George Thomas, the president of the University of Utah, who had personally and vigorously recruited Gillin to fill the lion-sized void left by the departure of anthropologist Julian H. Steward. There are few clues as to why a university president expended so much energy wooing Gillin when there were probably other candidates more experienced in the archaeology of the Great Basin and Colorado Plateau. Gillin was, at the time, relatively unknown, a young man who hailed from a scholarly pedigree but otherwise was unseasoned in the archaeology of Utah or the West. He had earned a doctorate from Harvard University the year before with a dissertation titled "The Barama River Caribs of British Guiana" (Gillin 1934a)—hardly a topic of keen interest to most citizens of Utah.

But as head-scratching as the appointment might have seemed to casual observers of university politics, it proved to have a profound impact on the history of Utah archaeology. During Gillin's short tenure at the University of Utah—he abruptly resigned two years later to pursue his two real loves, sociology and anthropology—he investigated dozens of archaeological sites in almost every corner of the state, from St. George to Elsinore, from Tooele to Marysvale, from Ephraim to Delta (see Gillin 1941). But it was Gillin's brief report of his excavations at Valley Village and Sky House in Nine Mile Canyon (Gillin 1938) that firmly placed the young scholar in the pantheon of eminent researchers—Noel Morss, Donald Scott, and Julian Steward—who had earlier ventured into Nine Mile Canyon, only to

OPPOSITE, State map of Utah.

recognize that the archaeology here was perplexingly different from what they had seen elsewhere in Utah and not easily explainable.

Gillin's investigations in Nine Mile Canyon stand today as a hallmark of sound scientific methods, meticulous attention to detail, and prompt publication. And although the canyon had been known to archaeologists for more than four decades before Gillin stepped foot there, his was the first scientific publication to address the remarkable resources of the canyon in any considerable depth. He was the first student of the canyon to collect wood samples that could be cross-referenced to tree-ring indices, which eventually resulted in the first temporal range for the Fremont culture, from about AD 950 to 1150. And Gillin's *Archaeological Investigations in Nine Mile Canyon, Utah (During the Year 1936)*, although tantalizingly brief, can be credited with exposing Nine Mile Canyon as a national archaeological treasure far richer than the myriad rock art sites that have fascinated chroniclers of eastern Utah. It is impossible today to discuss the ancient peoples of Nine Mile Canyon without homage to the foundation laid by Gillin more than 75 years ago.

Gillin was not the first researcher to venture into Nine Mile Canyon, and most certainly he was not the last. But his arrival there marked a nexus, of sorts, between the past and the present. As discussed in Chapters 1 and 2, the history of archaeological inquiry in Nine Mile Canyon mirrors that in Utah as a whole. It began with the landmark U.S. government surveys of Powell, King, and Hayden in the 1870s and 1880s, all of which fostered a keen public appetite for information about the mysterious lost cultures of the West. By the 1890s and early 1900s, archaeology, not yet a scientific discipline, had become the domain of Renaissance men— inquisitive scholars trained in geology, ethnology, linguistics, and the classic arts—who were more attuned to colorful speculation and impressive artifact collections than they were to understanding the people who left them behind.

By the late 1920s and early 1930s, archaeology had begun to emerge as a discipline in its own right, inspired in large part by Alfred V. Kidder and his colleagues at Harvard University, many of whom would focus their attention on Nine Mile Canyon in those years. In Chapter 3, we'll see how their investigations led directly to the Fremont culture concept still employed by archaeologists today—that the prehistoric agriculturalists north of the Colorado River were similar to but different from their Ancestral Puebloan contemporaries south of the river. Unfortunately, most of the field notes and photographs stemming from this work remained unpublished and forgotten for more than three decades; some have never been published.

The Harvard University investigations marked a watershed moment in Utah archaeology. But the transition to more exacting scientific standards did not go unchallenged. In Chapter 4, we'll meet a cadre of amateur archaeologists who worked in direct competition with university scholars in Nine Mile Canyon. Although not trained in archaeological techniques, they conducted excavations, acquired collections of artifacts, and published their findings in scores of articles in the various natural history journals common at that time. Quite simply, there were no laws or standards requiring any level of education or training. Some of the amateur archaeologists were conscientious and attempted to hold themselves to scientific standards. Others were little more than glorified looters.

When John Gillin arrived at the University of Utah in 1935, he was immediately tasked with implementing the state's first law protecting archaeological resources. Gillin established requirements that all archaeological research must be conducted under the auspices of state permits issued only to qualified archaeologists, and that archaeologists must publish their findings promptly (see Chapter 5). He founded the University of Utah Museum as the central repository for not only the artifacts collected but the reports generated by the researchers. These standards were overtly intended to thwart the vandalism and looting so rampant at the time. Whether intended or not, the rules were a direct slap at the scores of university scholars who had excavated Utah sites, hauled away artifacts, and never published their findings. And Gillin's regulations brought an end to the era of the amateur archaeologist. Gillin's investigations in Nine Mile Canyon may have been the first in Utah conducted under this regulatory framework—one that is largely intact today.

Gillin's departure from the University of Utah also marked a hiatus of academic interest in Nine Mile Canyon. James Gunnerson made only a passing reference to the canyon during his "statewide" survey in 1954, and not until 1975 was the canyon revisited, this time by a team of students from Brigham Young University. As we see in Chapter 6, not until 1989 would the canyon again become the focus of serious researchers, through a three-year field school carried out by Brigham Young University and a decade-long inventory conducted by dedicated amateurs working alongside professional archaeologists. Collectively, these efforts culminated in the first systematic examination of specific areas of the canyon, demonstrating an exceptionally high density of rock art sites, perhaps the greatest concentration anywhere in North America, earning it the moniker "World's Longest Art Gallery."

Archaeological research in Nine Mile Canyon has experienced another renaissance in the 2000s. Due to the discovery of massive natural gas deposits on the plateau above the canyon, investigations mandated under the National Historic Preservation Act have resulted in research into little-known and poorly understood areas at higher elevations. And the nonprofit Colorado Plateau Archaeological Alliance, seeking to understand the cumulative effects of development on fragile archaeological sites, has conducted comprehensive surveys of entire blocks in the canyon bottom. Sites have been excavated, radiocarbon dates have been reported, and archaeologists have a much better understanding today about how the prehistoric inhabitants of Nine Mile Canyon incorporated the entire landscape into a lifeway uniquely adapted to this harsh and arid environment (see Chapter 7).

Published in 1938, Gillin's *Archaeological Investigations in Nine Mile Canyon (During the Year 1936)* was a watershed moment in the history of archaeological research in Nine Mile Canyon, and its significance has only grown as scholars have built on its initial framework of ideas. In 1955, the report was republished by the University of Utah Press under the title *Archeological Investigations in Nine Mile Canyon: A Re-publication.* As an acknowledgment that Gillin's research has stood the test of time, 75 years after the original was published it is available again online as part of the University of Utah Press's Open Access Collection hosted by the Marriott Library.

This book is foremost a history of the archaeologists—myself included—who have ventured into Nine Mile Canyon, only to become bewildered at the puzzling archaeology there. We don't understand it fully, but we are making strides. And because of the unprecedented amount of research now being done, our understanding of the ancient people who lived there is changing with each new discovery. In the foreword to the 1955 reprint of Gillin's publication, editor Robert Anderson observed that Nine Mile Canyon is a "key to Basin history which offers great possibilities and which has not yet been fully exploited." That is still true today. But Nine Mile Canyon could soon become one of Utah's most studied and, we hope, best-understood archaeological regions.

1

John Wesley Powell and the Conundrum of Nine Mile Canyon

Left [Beaman] at the mouth of Nine Mile Creek, a beautiful little clear stream about a rod wide, coming in from the west. It has considerable water now, showing that it must be fed by springs.

—Journal of Almon Harris Thompson, August 17, 1871

Context and Conundrums

Nine Mile Canyon is a serpentine jewel situated on the northern edge of the West Tavaputs Plateau, itself a rugged landscape of arid canyons that defies most attempts to tame the wilderness with roads and ranches. Even with the rush to harvest vast natural gas reserves deep below the plateau crust, most of this largely waterless region in eastern Utah remains unknown to all but a handful of the hardiest cowboys, those with intimate knowledge of the few horse trails in and out of the labyrinth, canyons that today bear names like Snap Canyon and Trail Canyon and Rock House. It is, in the words of famed nineteenth-century explorer John Wesley Powell, "a region of wildest desolation" (Powell 1961:191).

Carved majestically into the soft Tertiary-age deposits of the Green River formation, the verdant valley that is Nine Mile Canyon stands in stark contrast to most of the parched West Tavaputs Plateau. The creek is a predictable and consistent source of flowing water even during the worst droughts, and even after quenching the thirst of the pastures and alfalfa fields along the floodplain. Trending west to east to its confluence with the Green River, the canyon is easily accessible from the many side drainages, some leading northward toward the Uinta Basin, others south toward the forested West Tavaputs Plateau, a highland Eden rich in elk, deer, bears, bighorn sheep, and cougars.

In all likelihood, the canyon was an ideal route for prehistoric peoples moving between the Uinta Basin to the north and the San Rafael Swell to the south—a natural corridor later recognized by the first Euroamericans in the region. In 1886, the U.S. Army constructed a freight road through the canyon, linking the Uinta Basin to railheads at Price, officially to service the military garrison at Fort Duchesne but more practically to foster

OPPOSITE, Nine Mile Canyon in the fall. Photo by Ray Boren.

ABOVE, Beauty amid the grandeur. Photo by Ray Boren.

Nine Mile Creek in the fall.
Photo by Ray Boren.

the economic development of a rare hydrocarbon called Gilsonite that was in great demand at that time (Geary 1981). Today all but the lower 10 miles of Nine Mile Canyon are accessible to tourists in cars and to fleets of 16-wheeled semi-trucks servicing the gas wells on the plateau above.

What's in a Name?

The name Nine Mile Creek first appears in the 1871 journals of participants in Major John Wesley Powell's second expedition down the Green and Colorado Rivers, many of whom were keenly interested in the prehistoric peoples of the region. The earliest reference to the archaeology of a canyon called Nine Mile is found in those journals.

But Nine Mile Canyon is unquestionably a misnomer. From its confluence with the Green River on the east to the point where the main creek diverges into two major branches is about 45 miles, and from there to the headwaters it extends another 20 miles or so. And therein is one of the greatest mysteries of Nine Mile Canyon: How did the canyon get its rather paradoxical name? There are plenty of local folk tales and even more assertions of fact that cannot be substantiated. According to *Utah Place Names: A Comprehensive Guide to the Origins of Geographic Names* (Van Cott 1990), the canyon was so named because it is 9 miles long—a spurious claim indeed.

Another legend has it that W. A. Miles settled the canyon with his wife and seven daughters, hence the "nine Miles" (Geary 1981). And while the Miles family is intertwined with the history of the region, the drainage was known as "Nine Mile" years before the Miles family arrived. Most accounts today, repeated authoritatively through scores of Internet postings about the canyon, attribute the name to Captain Francis Marion Bishop, a cartographer on Powell's Colorado River Exploring Expedition of 1871 (his participation is frequently and erroneously attributed to the 1869 expedition). According to the official Bureau of Land Management website for the canyon, Bishop "used a nine-mile transect for mapping the canyon," and hence he is responsible for the canyon's name (Bureau of Land Management 2008).

Powell Slept Here

Did Powell know of Nine Mile Canyon? The only reference in the expedition journals to a possible mapping triangulation was Bishop's obscure "I was up on the cliff taking the topography of the creek" (1947:189). But there is no mistaking the fact that the 1871 expedition journals referred to a Nine Mile Creek, and a later 1875 profile map resulting from the expedition marks the first topographical reference to a creek by that name (Powell 1879; see also map on p. 4). During the course of recent archaeological research along the Desolation Canyon portion of the Green River (see map on p. 4), the Colorado Plateau Archaeological Alliance set out to

ABOVE, Deer grazing in the pastures along Nine Mile Creek. Photo by Ray Boren.

BELOW, Francis Marion Bishop in about 1872, while a member of John Wesley Powell's Colorado River Exploring Expedition. Used by permission, Utah State Historical Society, all rights reserved.

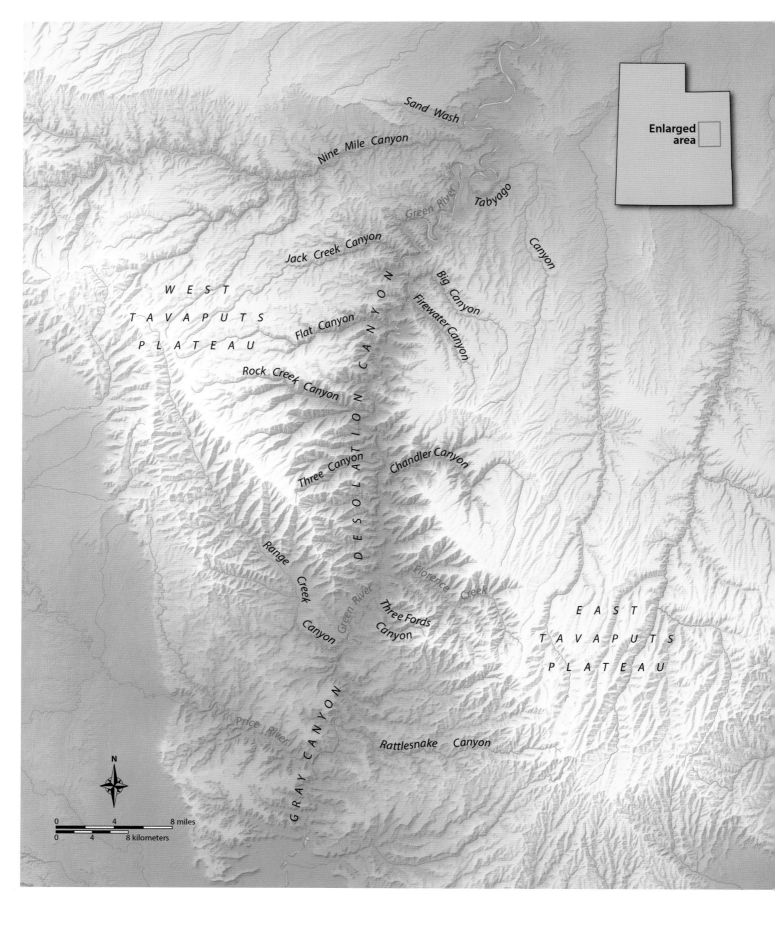

Sand Wash

Nine Mile Canyon

Green River

Tabyago

Canyon

Jack Creek Canyon

Big Canyon

WEST

Firewater Canyon

TAVAPUTS

Flat Canyon

PLATEAU

DESOLATION CANYON

Rock Creek Canyon

Three Canyon

Chandler Canyon

Range

Creek

Florence

Canyon

Green River

Creek

EAST

Three Fords

TAVAPUTS

Canyon

PLATEAU

GRAY CANYON

Price River

Rattlesnake Canyon

N

0   4   8 miles

0   4   8 kilometers

Enlarged area

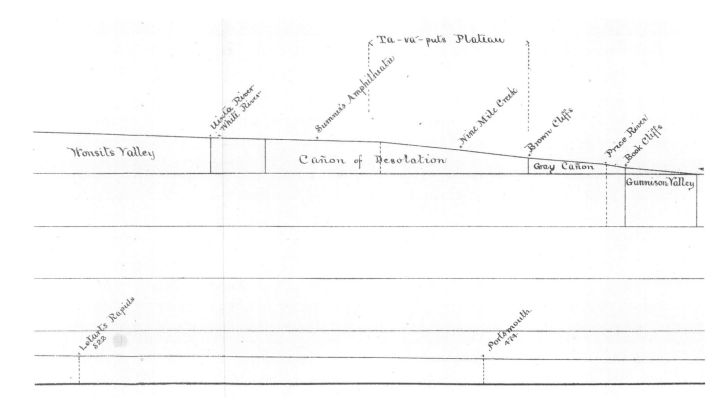

Ta-va-puts Plateau

Uinta River / White River   Sumner's Amphitheatre   Nine Mile Creek   Brown Cliffs   Price River / Book Cliffs

Wonsits Valley

Cañon of Desolation

Gray Cañon

Gunnison Valley

Letarts Rapids 522

Portsmouth 474

identify the camp locations of the 1871 expedition throughout Desolation Canyon, using clues in the journal accounts and the 1871 photographs of E. O. Beaman (see Spangler, Aton, and Spangler 2007). Working from a known location, researchers could move forward and backward from each datum using the estimated mileages in the journals, descriptions of the local landscape, and historic photographs.

Two expedition landmarks along the route were known with a high degree of certainty: Sumner's Amphitheatre and Lighthouse Rock, both of them established from 1871 photos. Other landmarks, such as Fretwater Falls, Log Cabin, and Price River, were known with a fairly high degree of certainty, based on good descriptions in the journals (the journals also referenced photographs at those locations but these have not been identified). And, of course, Nine Mile Creek was a known topographic feature mentioned in the journals. These places retain the same names today that were first applied by members of the Powell expedition, many of them by Frederick Dellenbaugh, a 17-year-old journalist who offered the richest written account of the 1871 adventures down the Green River (Dellenbaugh 1908; see also Darrah 1951).

This liberal application of deductive reasoning, which required a detailed reading and rereading of the journals, worked very well, and in

ABOVE, Profile map produced for J. W. Powell's *Arid Lands Report* (Powell 1879). Note the location of Nine Mile Creek below (south) of Sumner's Amphitheatre.

OPPOSITE, Topographic map of the Tavaputs Plateau with major drainages. Nine Mile Canyon is near the top and Range Creek is near the bottom.

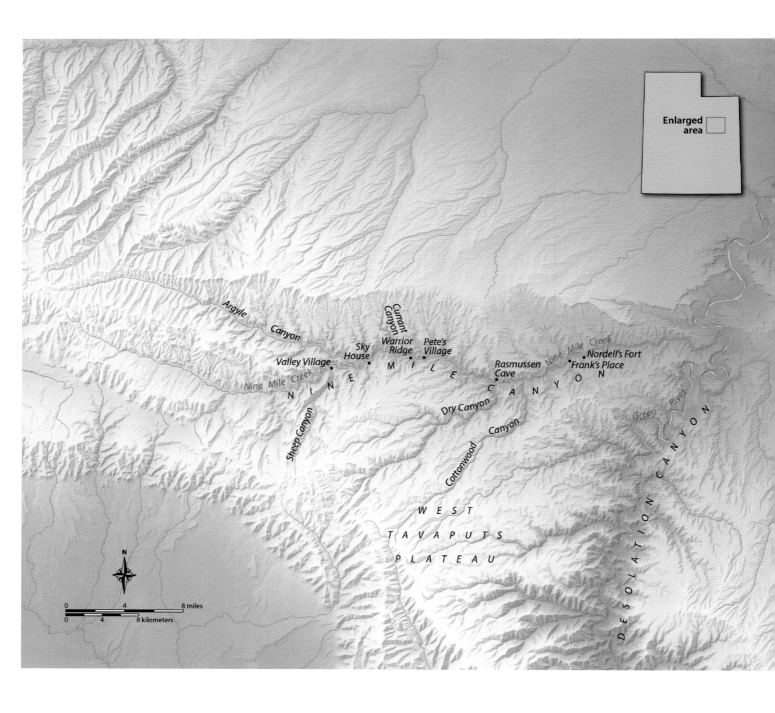

Argyle Canyon

Currant Canyon

Sky House

Warrior Ridge

Pete's Village

Valley Village

Nordell's Fort

Rasmussen Cave

Frank's Place

Nine Mile Creek

Nine Mile Creek

N I N E   M I L E   C A N Y O N

Sheep Canyon

Dry Canyon

Cottonwood Canyon

Green River

D E S O L A T I O N   C A N Y O N

W E S T
T A V A P U T S
P L A T E A U

N

0   4   8 miles
0   4   8 kilometers

Enlarged area

Sumner's Amphitheatre as it appeared in 1871. This topographic feature is located downriver (south) from the mouth of Nine Mile Canyon. Photo by E. O. Beaman. J. K. Hillers Collection, U.S. Geological Survey.

OPPOSITE, Topographic map of the West Tavaputs Plateau and Nine Mile Canyon, with major canyons and archaeological sites.

most instances the locations of the expedition camps could be narrowed to a specific area. But there was one notable exception. The Nine Mile Creek referred to in the journals seemed to be located about 42 miles farther downriver than it is today. The unavoidable conclusion is that the Nine Mile Creek in the journals is, in fact, known today as Rock Creek, and the expedition seems to have passed today's Nine Mile Creek without comment (and without any nine-mile triangulations).

Debunking the Nine Mile triangulation myth begins with journal entries for August 8, 1871, when the expedition arrived at a camp about 32 miles below the Duchesne River (it was known as the Uinta River in 1871). Some of the journalists described a vast amphitheater where the river doubled back on itself. And they wrote about considerable efforts over parts of three days to obtain photographs of this remarkable feature. Only Dellenbaugh's account, written many years later, refers to a name for this feature: "It was named Sumner's Amphitheatre after Jack Sumner

Lighthouse Rock as it appeared in 1871. Photo by E. O. Beaman. J. K. Hillers Collection, U.S. Geological Survey.

of the first expedition" (1908:79). Beaman's 1871 photographs of Sumner's Amphitheatre verify that this is the same topographic feature known by that name today. At this point, the expedition would have been about 11 miles *below* the mouth of today's Nine Mile Creek.

Later, on August 10, the expedition floated 10 or 11 miles downriver before camping for the night, commenting little on the local topography. This distance would have placed the camp somewhere in the Peter's Point area. Narrowing the location of this camp would likely be impossible if not for a single remark by Dellenbaugh that "opposite our next camp a pinnacle stood detached from the wall on a shelf high above the water suggesting a beacon, and it was named Lighthouse Rock" (1908:80). The presence of a pinnacle is corroborated by Beaman's 1871 photograph, which clearly depicts the same Lighthouse Rock landmark known to river runners today. This is roughly 24 miles below the mouth of today's Nine Mile Creek.

The first written references of any kind to Nine Mile Creek came a week later and roughly 42 miles below the mouth of today's Nine Mile Creek.

On August 15–16, the expedition was camped somewhere along the extensive flats at the mouth of Steer Ridge Canyon, perhaps above Surprise Rapid, located 40 miles below the mouth of today's Nine Mile Creek. The journal accounts are fairly consistent after this point as they collectively refer to a flowing stream they call Nine Mile Creek, beginning with entries for August 17.

Almon Harris Thompson, the commander of the expedition in the absence of John Wesley Powell, wrote, "Left Beaman ¾ of a mile up river to take views. He got some fine ones. Left him at the mouth of Nine Mile Creek, a beautiful little clear stream about a rod wide, coming in from the west. It has considerable water now, showing that it must be fed by springs" (1939:34). John Steward observed, "It is a beautiful little brook with about 2 feet of water that comes bubbling rapidly down the valley" (1948:219). Walter "Clem" Powell wrote that he and Beaman, and later with Thompson in tow, "all climbed the low foothills back of us. Had a fine view up the valley of Nine Mile Creek and of the different peaks. We concluded to leave the boxes on the bank of the creek and come up in the morning and take views. Drank some of its waters but found it strongly impregnated with alkali, though clear and cold" (1948:300).

The following day, August 18, Clem Powell wrote that he, Beaman, and "Jack" (probably John Hillers) returned to Nine Mile Creek, "shouldered the boxes and gallantly marched up the mountain. Took a couple of views, one looking up the creek's valley and one looking down the river. Came down, repacked the boxes, fixed the negatives, and went back to camp" (1948:300). While Beaman was taking photographs, Bishop, who did not accompany the photographers, wrote his obscure reference: "I was up on the cliff taking the topography of the creek" (1947:189). There is also a reference at this point to the collection of an arrowhead, perhaps the first artifact ever collected in this region with any scientific intent.

These journal accounts clearly demonstrate that the Nine Mile Creek described in 1871 is not the Nine Mile Creek of today, and that it is most certainly Rock Creek, the only permanent flowing water on the west side of the river between today's Nine Mile Creek, located 42 river miles to the north, and Range Creek, located another 22 miles to the south (see also map on p. 6). But this raises even more questions about the origins of the Nine Mile name. Unlike other landforms, to which the 1871 expedition

Almon Harris Thompson, commander of the 1871 Colorado River Exploring Expedition in Desolation Canyon and brother-in-law of Major John Wesley Powell. Photo by J. K. Hillers. J. K. Hillers Collection, U.S. Geological Survey.

Rock Creek as it appears today. The Powell expedition referred to this stream of clear, cold water as Nine Mile Creek. Photo by Dan Miller.

freely applied new names, like Fretwater Falls and Sumner's Amphitheatre, this location apparently already had a known place name: Steward wrote on August 17 that "we passed the mouth of a small stream... which we suppose to be what is known as Nine Mile Creek, that is said to pass not far from the Uinta Agency" (1948:219). Today's Rock Creek is nowhere near the Uinta Agency, whereas today's Nine Mile Creek is somewhat closer, about 30 miles south of the agency headquarters.

Could it be that Major John Wesley Powell, the expedition commander, who did not accompany the 1871 expedition during its adventures in Desolation Canyon, had merely told the participants to watch for "Nine Mile Creek"? Could they have mistaken the clear brook at Rock Creek for a similarly sized stream 42 miles upriver? Was today's Nine Mile Creek actually discovered and named during the 1869 expedition, and because none of the 1869 participants were along for the 1871 expedition through Desolation Canyon, was the real Nine Mile Creek simply missed? And if it was named in 1869, why was it tagged with that name, given that formal mapping triangulations were not part of the 1869 expedition's duties?

The journals of the 1869 expedition offer no clues. Neither of the two 1869 diarists, Jack Sumner (Sumner 1947) and George Y. Bradley (Bradley 1947), refers to Nine Mile Creek, or to any creek in the Desolation Canyon area, for that matter. Powell's journal (1947) is the most fragmentary of all, offering minimal description for reconstructing the expedition itinerary. A more detailed account is offered in Powell's later recollections in *The Exploration of the Colorado River and Its Tributaries* (Powell 1961), but it is flawed by his combination of notes and memories from both the 1869 and 1871 expeditions. Nonetheless, this account does not mention Nine Mile Creek.

A close reading of the various accounts suggests that neither the 1869 nor 1871 expeditions camped anywhere near the mouth of today's Nine Mile Canyon, nor did they stop there for mapping purposes. Quite simply, Francis Marion Bishop's "nine-mile triangulation" never occurred at the canyon that bears that name today. More likely, today's Nine Mile Creek went unnoticed by both expeditions. The expeditions also failed to note the presence of Range Creek lower on the Green River and the Escalante River lower on the Colorado River.

If the 1871 participants were mistaken in their identification of Nine Mile Creek, there is no supporting documentation that the Nine Mile Creek of today was called by that name at that time. So if today's Nine Mile Creek is not the Nine Mile Creek of the Powell expeditions, what was its name at that time? Some historians believe Nine Mile Creek may be the Euwinty River referred to in the 1825 journals of William Ashley (Morgan 1955, 1964; Gowans 1985; Smith 1987). By 1866, a General Land Office map of Utah shows a stream labeled White River in the approximate location of Nine Mile Creek, as well as another nearby White River in the approximate location of the Price River (the latter was commonly known as the White River at the time of the Powell expeditions). It is not a huge leap to suggest that "White" is an Anglo modification of "Euwinty," but it is speculative nonetheless. It could just as easily be read as "Uinta."

Major John Wesley Powell (*right*) in southern Utah in about 1870. J. K. Hillers Collection, U.S. Geological Survey.

Minnie Maud Creek

The name Nine Mile Creek was first published in a profile map attached to Powell's report to Congress of his 1869, 1871, and 1872 expeditions (Powell 1879; see map on p. 4), but its location is clearly marked below Sumner's Amphitheatre, not in its current location above that landmark. In fact, there are no references to any creeks in Desolation Canyon above Sumner's

The canyon walls of Nine Mile. Photo by Ray Boren.

Amphitheatre. Adding even more confusion, A. H. Thompson briefly described today's Nine Mile Creek in Powell's *Report on the Lands of the Arid Region*. But he called the creek Minnie Maud, a name now reserved for the upper north fork of Nine Mile Creek. Thompson certainly knew that Nine Mile Creek, as described by the 1871 diarists, was much lower in Desolation Canyon. So he, or Powell, applied the name Minnie Maud to the stream to the north. Thompson described water-flow tests of Minnie Maud Creek in 1877 that yielded 16 cubic feet per second, suggesting that the canyon had become known to government surveyors at about the same time or somewhat earlier than the first Euroamerican settlers in the canyon in the late 1870s (Thompson, in Powell 1879:159–160).

The origins of the name Minnie Maud are likewise clouded in local lore. Geary cites local accounts of an aboriginal origin that is sometimes spelled "Minniemaud," but there is no citation for the source of that information

(Geary 1981). Another account has it that the canyon was named for twin sisters, Minnie and Maud Hall, who were born in Escalante, Utah, in 1893 and moved to the canyon a few years later (*Sun Advocate* 1970), although this also occurred long after the creek already carried the Minnie Maud name.

Another popular account suggests that Major Powell named the creek for two relatives, Minnie and Maud, and there appears to be some support for this particular legend, albeit with revisions. A review of records at FamilySearch.org found that Major Powell's brother, William Bramwell "Bram" Powell, married Wilhelmina Paul Bengelstraeter. Wilhelmina went by the name Minnie. They had a daughter, Maud, born August 22, 1867, in Peru, Illinois. No reference was found in the database that Maud went by Minnie Maud, but according to Maud's biographer, Karen A. Shaffer, her actual given name was Minnie Maud, though she later dropped the Minnie (personal communication, 2010).

According to Donald Worster's authoritative biography of Major Powell, Maud was a child prodigy on the violin, debuting with the New York Philharmonic Society at the age of sixteen. She formed her own Maud Powell String Quartet and, from a base in London, played the leading concert halls of Europe, becoming one of the most renowned string artists of her day. Uncle Wes, immensely proud of his talented niece, followed her

Minnie Maud Powell, niece of John Wesley Powell and the original namesake of the creek that flows in what is today Nine Mile Canyon. Photo courtesy of the Maud Powell Society for Music and Education, Brevard, North Carolina.

career closely" (Worster 2001:548). She would have been about 10 years old and first emerging as an acclaimed child violinist in Illinois when the creek in eastern Utah came to bear her name.

Major Powell's fondness for his accomplished niece apparently continued in the decades that followed, even though fame spirited Maud away to London and the major to Washington, D.C., where he later directed the Bureau of Ethnology and the U.S. Geological Survey. When Bram Powell also later moved to Washington, D.C., to become superintendent of public schools, Maud was a frequent visitor to her uncle's house on M Street, where she entertained Washington's scientific and political elite with her musical virtuosity (Shaffer and Greenwood 1988).

If the Minnie Maud name can be attributed to Major Powell's affection for his favorite niece, then this name was probably applied in about 1877 or 1878 during preparation of the seminal *Report on the Lands of the Arid Region* (first released in 1878, but revised, corrected, and re-released in 1879 as the formal report available today) and during preparation of the map that accompanied it. This map uses the name Minnie Maud for the creek but applies the name Nine Mile Valley to the upper south fork of Minnie Maud Creek.

The fact he did not use the name Nine Mile Creek for this stream implies that Powell recognized a distinction between Minnie Maud Creek on the north and Nine Mile Creek (today's Rock Creek) on the south, although the latter is not mentioned anywhere in the *Report*. It can also be inferred that today's Nine Mile Canyon, explored and tested for its water potential in 1877, was unnamed at the time of the Colorado River Exploring Expeditions of 1869 and 1871, and that it was probably unknown to the participants, thereby requiring a new appellation in which Powell honored his niece. It would also support the contention that Rock Creek today is and was the Nine Mile Creek of the 1871 Colorado River Exploring Expedition.

So how did the name Nine Mile Creek get transferred forty-some miles to the north to a creek that was unknown in 1869 and 1871? It is quite possible that those creating maps in the late nineteenth century mistakenly placed the name Nine Mile Creek on a stream far to the north of where the explorers had actually described it. Throughout time, the canyon became known as Nine Mile Canyon and the creek as Minnie

The lush high plateau above Nine Mile Canyon. Photo by Ray Boren.

Maud Creek. Eventually, it evolved into Nine Mile Creek and Nine Mile Canyon, with the Minnie Maud name reserved for the northern tributary.

In other words, the Nine Mile name, as used today, is a grand case of mistaken identity that ultimately frustrated Major Powell's efforts to recognize his niece, Minnie Maud. Mistakes aside, when the first archaeologists arrived here in 1892, the canyon had already become known as Nine Mile Canyon.

Note: A version of this chapter, titled "Nine Mile, Minnie Maud and the Mystery of a Place Name," appeared in *Utah Historical Quarterly* 79, no. 1 (2011).

Utah, being on the outskirts of the country occupied by a great nation whose headquarters were probably in Mexico, might properly be expected to be provided with a considerable number of military posts or watch stations such as those herein described. —HENRY MONTGOMERY, 1894

Discovering Nine Mile: The First Archaeologists

The ancient ruins and rock art of Utah have long evoked fascination among Euroamericans, whose settlement of the region in the mid-1800s occurred centuries after the myriad cliff dwellings and pithouse communities had been abandoned. Who were these people who had simply vanished? Why had they, in some cases, left their dwellings stocked with pottery and clothing as if they intended to return any day? In some instances, the charred remains of buildings and gruesome dismemberment evident in the human burials evoked images of violence and annihilation. Given the human propensity to assign names, the ancients were sometimes referred to as Tehuas by the Spanish and as Shinumos or Moquis by the first American explorers and settlers of the region.

As people everywhere are prone to do, those who discover the mysterious remnants of lost peoples commonly interpret the unknown through the prism of their own world view. And among the immigrants who began to arrive in the Salt Lake Valley in 1847, and who over the next three decades would settle every corner of the state, the ubiquitous archaeological remains were seen as evidence of the lost civilizations described in The Book of Mormon, the sacred tome of the Mormon faithful.

Although written accounts of the first observations of Utah's prehistoric remains are indeed rare, it is clear that nineteenth-century immigrants were keenly aware they were not the first to make their homes here. Frederick Dellenbaugh, a journalist on John Wesley Powell's 1871 and 1872 Colorado River expeditions and a repeat visitor to the Kanab area for many years afterward, noted that local residents were actively digging into prehistoric sites for artifacts, either for sale or for personal collections.

OPPOSITE, Portion of the famous Owl Panel in middle Nine Mile Canyon. Photo by Ray Boren.

Characteristic rock art of Nine Mile Canyon. Photo by Ray Boren.

There is scarcely a settlement in all Utah that is not on or near the site of an ancient village; and it seems unjust that the few antiquities that are left should be carelessly destroyed. Often, a settler who knows nothing about the Shinumos, and who cares less, finds on his land a mound covered with regular slabs that are just the thing for building a chimney, or a wall, or something of that sort. So he tears the mound to pieces and uses what is desirable. If he runs across a lot of pots, he examines them with some curiosity and sends them into his house. In a few weeks the fragments may be found in the back yard. Should he stumble upon a skeleton, he is at first somewhat amazed; but always considering a dead "injun" worthy of unlimited respect, he tenderly gathers the bones together and digs for them a new grave. Occasionally, a settlement contains an individual who has gained some knowledge of such things; and if he happens to be the possessor of any relics he puts upon them no modest price [1877:178–179].

Dellenbaugh's observations are probably applicable to Nine Mile Canyon, where settlers began to arrive in earnest after 1886, when the U.S. military constructed a freight road through the canyon to link Fort Duchesne to railheads at Price (Geary 1981). Early exploration of the many ruins of Nine Mile Canyon and the removal of artifacts, for personal collections or for sale, probably occurred at that same time, although written accounts of such activities have not yet surfaced. It is certain, though, that the archaeological riches here had become widely known by 1892, when the first archaeological expeditions ventured into the canyon.

To properly understand how those first settlers viewed the prehistoric past around them requires historical context, in particular the evolution of scientific thought in the nineteenth century and religious reactions to it. When Brigham Young arrived in the Salt Lake Valley in 1847, archaeology had not yet emerged as a discipline in its own right. Rather, it was the domain of intellectuals and "arm-chair antiquarians" who speculated endlessly on the origins and demise of the ancients and who in some cases funded excavations to acquire artifacts for private collections (Willey and Sabloff 1980). There was little, if any, science behind these excavations, which were tantamount to the wholesale destruction of entire sites in the pursuit of valuable antiquities.

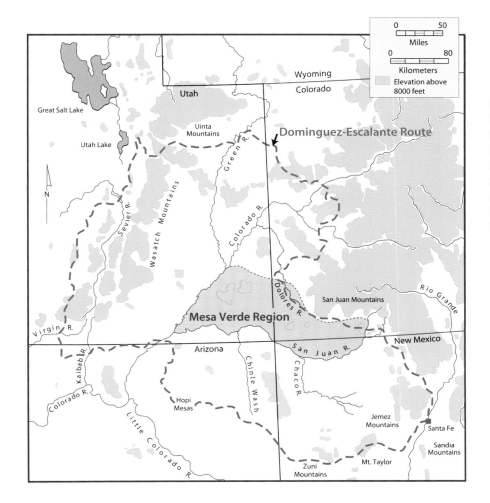

General route of the Domínguez-Escalante Expedition from Santa Fe through western Colorado and northern Utah. Nine Mile Canyon is near the upper limit of the route. Image used with permission of the Crow Canyon Archaeological Center, Cortez, Colorado.

The nineteenth-century antiquarian interest in American archaeology was fueled in part by the written accounts of relatively well educated Spanish friars, who commonly interpreted the religions and customs of Native Americans as "corrupt and distorted versions of the true religion and morality that God had revealed to Adam and his descendants" (Trigger 1989:65). This assessment was later shared by Mormon arrivals to Utah, albeit with modifications unique to The Book of Mormon.

Religious biases aside, most of the Catholic friars were influenced by trends in European scientific inquiry that required detailed descriptions of indigenous peoples and their ancestors (Trigger 1989). And this was certainly true of the first Spanish *entrada* into Utah in 1776, when Fray Francisco Atanasio Domínguez and Fray Silvestre Vélez de Escalante explored a northern route from Santa Fe to the recently established garrison of Monterey on the California coast. Their route took them north through western Colorado and then west through northern Utah, passing about 40 miles north of Nine Mile Canyon and eventually traveling on to

Sculpture at This Is the Place State Park honoring the arrival of the Spanish friars at Utah Lake. Photo by Ray Boren.

Utah Lake (see map on p. 19). On September 17, 1776, while following the Duchesne River upstream, Escalante wrote, "We saw ruins near it of a very ancient pueblo where there were fragments of stones for grinding maize, of jars, and of pots of clay. The pueblo's shape was circular, as indicated by the ruins now almost completely in mounds" (in Warner 1976:47).

Escalante's journal reflects a genuine interest in aboriginal peoples, and he may have been the first to compare prehistoric remains of the northern Colorado Plateau with those of the native peoples then living in the area (archaeologists call it ethnographic analogy). Escalante compared rock art styles found in northwestern Colorado with those of the Apache peoples at that time. And the ancient pottery was similar to that of the Puebloan peoples living in New Mexico. Escalante wrote, "The land by way of which the Tihuas, Tehuas and the other Indians transmigrated to this kingdom; which is clearly shown by the ruins of the pueblos which I have seen in it, whose form was the same that they afterwards gave to theirs in New Mexico; and the fragments of clay and pottery which I also saw in the said country are much like that which the said Tehuas make today" (in Tyler 1951:195).

By the mid-nineteenth century, the period of European-influenced scientific inquiry had been replaced by a unique American hybrid of antiquarianism, evolutionism, and armchair speculation as to the origins of indigenous peoples. Throughout the nineteenth century, there was a general rise in the appreciation of sciences in general as America pushed ever deeper into unexplored and often exotic regions of the continent, creating "an intellectual climate in which anthropology and archaeology could flourish" (Willey and Sabloff 1980:4). Archaeological inquiry during this period was greatly influenced by the publication in 1859 of Charles Darwin's *On the Origin of Species*, the florescence of geology as a scientific discipline, and a resurgence of scientific thought at the expense of theological dogma (Willey and Sabloff 1980:34). It was within this intellectual environment that landmark surveys of the northern Colorado Plateau and Great Basin were conducted by explorers John C. Fremont, Howard Stansbury, Clarence King, Ferdinand Hayden, John Wesley Powell, George M. Wheeler, E. G. Beckwith, and John W. Gunnison, all among the most famous explorers of the American West. These expeditions were conducted in anticipation of a great western migration that would open North America to settlement.

Most of the expeditions passing through Utah made some reference to the ancients long vanished or to the native peoples then inhabiting the country. For example, on August 5, 1871, while the Colorado River Exploring Expedition was camped just upriver from the mouth of Nine Mile Canyon, participant John Steward wrote in his journal of the discovery of two Indian graves.

Fall tranquillity in Nine Mile Canyon. Photo by Ray Boren.

They may be those of the Moquis tribes which evidently inhabited this section of the country at some time and were driven out many years ago. Their ruins are everywhere to be found where the country is rendered inhabitable by garden spots along the river. Their houses were built of stone, which is something unusual with Indian tribes. Several of their mills for grinding corn were found by the boys on their way to Uinta; their inscriptions were on the cliffs in many places. We found a fine group of them upon the lower sandstone cliffs at the mouth of

John Steward, who participated in Major Powell's explorations of the Green and Colorado Rivers, was a keen observer of Utah archaeology. J. K. Hillers Collection, U.S. Geological Survey.

Craggy Canyon. It is possible, however, they were all made by Indians belonging to some other tribe. The Moquis are far superior to the Utes, who call them "wisemen" when speaking of them. The Utes claim their forefathers conquered and drove them away [Steward 1948:211].

The rise of geology as a science had profound influence on scientific inquiry in Utah, with Powell, King, and Hayden—the greatest of the Utah explorers of that era—emerging as the nation's preeminent geologists during the latter half of the nineteenth century. In the absence of archaeology as a distinct discipline, the description of archaeological remains often fell to those trained in geology. And while the surveys headed by Powell, King, and Hayden all made archaeological observations in Utah, the origins of archaeological inquiry here are instead rooted in the investigations of three more obscure individuals: Edward Palmer, a medical doctor and respected botanist, and Don Maguire and Henry Montgomery, who were trained in geology but who had an abiding love of archaeology. The latter two would figure prominently in the history of Nine Mile Canyon.

The Botanist Archaeologist

Fueled by a series of public lectures and journal articles, John Wesley Powell's prominence in the scientific community of Washington, D.C., reached unprecedented heights in the early 1870s. In 1874, renowned ornithologist Spencer Baird, at that time assistant secretary of the Smithsonian Institution, enlisted Powell's support to plan the 1876 Centennial Exposition in Philadelphia. Also notable in these plans was Frederic Putnam of the Peabody Museum, a veteran of George Wheeler's topographic surveys in the West (see Putnam 1879) and a leading figure in the still-emerging science of archaeology. Their plans included an extensive display of ethnographic and archaeological artifacts from North American Indians that had been collected by various government surveys operating throughout the western territories (Fowler and Matley 1978:20; McVaugh 1956:68).

Among the up-and-coming scientists recruited to assist with collections for the Centennial Exposition was Edward Palmer, a medical doctor and Civil War veteran who had attracted the attention of the Smithsonian and

LEFT, Typical Fremont petroglyphs. Note the human figures lying sideways. Photo by Ray Boren.

RIGHT, This panel is often called "Balloon Man" or "The Juggler." Photo by Ray Boren.

the Peabody Museum by virtue of the botanical collections he had made in Paraguay, Kansas, Nebraska, and Colorado. A product of the insatiable national interest in the natural sciences, Palmer found himself enveloped in a scientific climate of collection and description, although he was more efficient in the former than the latter. Baird apparently had discussed with Palmer the possibility of making archaeological and ethnographic collections for the Smithsonian. At the same time, Putnam had engaged his services to make collections on behalf of the Peabody Museum. In a letter written in the fall of 1875, Baird told Palmer, "Do not fail to let me have the refusal of anything you collect in the line of ethnology," and in another letter about the same time he stated, "I need not tell you to pay particular attention to the subject of foods of the Indians wherever you go as this has always attracted your attention. I would, however, ask you to inquire into all the special methods for taking fish and game, getting hooks, lines, nets, etc." (in Fowler and Matley 1978:20).

Palmer arrived in Utah in the fall of 1875 and immediately began a series of archaeological excavations in the Santa Clara River area near St. George and, later that year, at a rockshelter near Kanab. His base of operations was the St. George residence of Joseph Ellis Johnson, a Mormon who had distinguished himself locally as a horticulturalist and whose family connections afforded him opportunities to explore archaeological sites on various properties. Palmer's excavations, although focused on the acquisition of

Ruins such as these are located on the steepest of canyon slopes. Photo by Ray Boren.

artifacts, were apparently conducted with precision and attention to detail, something unusual at the time. Johnson's son, Charles,

> helped in the excavations. He [said] that Dr. Palmer watched like the proverbial hawk each removal of articles from the burial places. The boys never had the slightest chance to snitch any choice bit for themselves. The things were brought over from the Santa Clara fields to the [Johnson family] library, where they were laid out on a long table. From here they were carefully packed and shipped by stagecoach to the railroad [Rosemary Johnson, in McVaugh 1956:65–66].

That is consistent with Palmer's own account contained in a letter written to Baird in October 1875, in which he described his meticulous methods: "I personally superintend the whole thing, taking out the specimens, saving every piece of those broken at once pasting the perfect ones with paper and wrapping the pieces of the broken pottery so that their edges do not rub and that none be lost" (in Fowler and Matley 1978:20). Palmer subsequently offered good descriptions of the materials he had removed, including ceramics, human burials, stone artifacts, fragments of textiles and leather, and shell and turquoise artifacts (Palmer 1876; see also Holmes 1886:287–288). Palmer's efforts in 1875 could very well be the first time a Utah archaeological site was excavated with scientific intent. And through a brief account in the *American Naturalist*, Palmer may have been the first to publish his findings (1876).

Palmer left Utah in early 1876 but returned in December of that year under the auspices of the Peabody Museum at Harvard University, the same institution that would later play such a prominent role in the archaeology of Nine Mile Canyon. Throughout 1877, Palmer excavated mounds in the Washington, Paragonah, and Beaver areas and in Kane County—all in southwestern Utah, far removed from Nine Mile Canyon. He also spent two weeks excavating mounds at Spring Lake Villa near Payson. In addition to the archaeological excavations, Palmer made botanical collections in the areas of St. Thomas in Nevada; Mount Trumbull, Beaver Dam, and Mokiak Pass in Arizona; and at Paragonah, Beaver, and Mountain Meadows in Utah (McVaugh 1956:68; Palmer 1878). It is unknown whether

Palmer's archaeological collections were included in the Centennial Exposition, the reason that he was originally dispatched to Utah.

The Chicago World's Fair

American interest in prehistoric peoples of the western United States underwent a revival in the 1880s with the discovery and widespread reporting of spectacular cliff ruins at Mesa Verde, Colorado, and the recovery of fascinating relics from cave sites in southeastern Utah. At that time, archaeological efforts were focused largely on the acquisition of artifact collections that could be exhibited in eastern museums. Large museums such as the Peabody at Harvard University, the American Museum of Natural History in New York, and the Heye Foundation's Museum of the American Indian, also in New York, sponsored numerous expeditions specifically to gather impressive collections for display. This practice created a lucrative market for artifacts from independent collectors (Janetski 1997).

Warren K. Moorehead argued forcefully for more careful archaeological excavation techniques. Photo courtesy of the Ohio Historical Society.

In 1892, archaeologist Warren K. Moorehead, described in many modern accounts as the dean of American archaeology, decried the wanton collection of artifacts and the destruction of ancient ruins. He blamed a

> number of wealthy relic collectors in the East who have been corresponding with traders with a view of securing specimens from the caves and ruins. They do not care to make primitive man a study, but are mere curiosity hunters, such as ones seen about the ruins of a city swept by a cyclone or flood. They do an immense amount of damage by encouraging the taking of pottery and other objects by persons incapable of handling finds properly [Moorehead 1892:563; see Janetski 1997 for historical context].

Archaeology began to emerge as a scientific discipline within this environment. In 1891, Frederic Ward Putnam was named chief of the Department of Ethnology at the World's Columbian Exposition in Chicago, an unprecedented exhibit of aboriginal artifacts that would open to the public in October 1893. Putnam used his position to secure funding for "original research and exploration to enable... as much new scientific material as time would permit" (in Phillips 1993:110). He also demanded rigid methods for scientific excavation of archaeological sites.

Utah, at that time still a territory, was eager to demonstrate its membership in the nation of states. Politically, it was a volatile time in Utah, where more than 1,300 Mormon leaders had been imprisoned for their practice of plural marriage. Church property had been confiscated by the federal government, political and social conflicts between Mormons and their "gentile" neighbors were escalating, and Congress steadfastly refused to grant statehood. In 1890, LDS church president Wilford Woodruff issued a manifesto renouncing the practice of plural marriage, and in 1892 the church's governing body formally petitioned for amnesty (see *LDS Millennial Star* 1892, in Alter 1932:465–466).

With territorial leaders desperate for statehood (it would not come for another four years), the Chicago World's Fair afforded an opportunity for Utah to participate in a national event, standing equal with other states. In that context, Utah officials created the Utah Territorial World's Fair Commission and appointed Don Maguire of Ogden as chief of the Department of Archaeology and Ethnology. He was assigned the task of traveling the state to acquire artifacts for the Utah exhibit—something he did with considerable enthusiasm (Kelly 1933).

Dominick "Don" Maguire was born on June 13, 1852, in Vermont, the youngest of five sons whose Irish immigrant parents transplanted the family to Iowa when Don was a child. His father, John, claimed to be an Irish separatist with a price on his head, something that did not deter him from acquiring a small fortune in Iowa through land and livestock investments. In the early 1870s, John moved his family to Ogden, Utah, where the railroad had opened up opportunities for various business ventures. Don was a sagacious businessman, but one afflicted with wanderlust and political radicalism (he claimed to have plotted attempts to overthrow the emperor Maximilian in Mexico and the British Crown in Canada). He worked for a spell as a livestock buyer for the military, a packer for government expeditions, and a miner, the proceeds from which funded his education at a Franciscan college in Santa Barbara, where he studied engineering, mathematics, and languages. In the late 1870s, he led trading expeditions to Utah, Nevada, and Arizona, where he became enamored of prehistoric ruins. He

Dominick "Don" Maguire had an abiding love of Utah archaeology. Used by permission, Utah State Historical Society, all rights reserved.

frequently traveled the mining districts of the West, garnering a small fortune supplying the mining camps with basic necessities (Maguire 1997).

According to an obituary penned by renowned Utah historian Charles Kelly, Maguire was, for his day, a Renaissance man: he was well educated, a writer of poetry, a survivor of a bison stampede and Apache wounds, a collector of books, a fluent speaker of Arabic, and possessor of a remarkable memory that made him "an inexhaustible fund of historic and scientific information" (Kelly 1933:9). By the early 1890s, Don Maguire had become an immensely successful businessman. How he came to the attention E. A. McDaniels of the Utah World's Fair Commission is not known. In the only written account of Maguire's activities as chief of the Department of Archaeology and Ethnology, Maguire states that his appointment came on August 15, 1892 (Maguire 1894:105), a perplexing date given that he had already been excavating Utah ruins for two months. The June 27, 1892, edition of the *LDS Millennial Star* describes in colorful detail the work of Maguire and a Mr. Streville, also from Ogden, of excavating prehistoric mounds at Willard, north of Ogden, a community fortified by a wall that he called the ancient city of Cublick (in Alter 1932:469). At the time, this site was one of the largest in Utah, but it was later destroyed during construction of the Willard Bay reservoir.

According to the "Report of the Department of Ethnology, Utah World's Fair Commission," Maguire directed excavations at numerous places: 43 prehistoric mounds at Willard, a large prehistoric cemetery at Lake Shore west of Plain City, a site within the city limits of South Ogden, prehistoric mounds in Provo and Payson, sites along the Virgin and Santa Clara Rivers near St. George, cave sites and cliff dwellings in San Juan County, and a massive site near Cedar City that he called the Royal Palace of Paragonah (Maguire 1894:105–110). This last site had been excavated by various parties since at least 1872, when members of the Wheeler Expedition reported (and dug into) 400 to 500 mounds (Wheeler 1889). Maguire's excavation techniques probably did not adhere to Frederic Putnam's mandate that excavations be conducted carefully and methodically. At Paragonah, Maguire hired four men with two teams of horses and plows to expose artifacts in a mound 150 feet square and 9 feet high—perhaps the single largest prehistoric community known in Utah (1894:108).

Three-horned snake in middle Nine Mile Canyon. Photo by Ray Boren.

After Maguire's excavations in the southwest part of Utah, and while en route to San Juan County, in Utah's southeast corner, Maguire and expedition photographer James H. Crockwell took a long detour and "made a journey" through Nine Mile Canyon, "where exist extensive remains of the Cliff Dwellers. Of these stone houses in the mountain declivities I obtained photographic views and from the interior much of the remains of the ancient inhabitants, such as broken pottery, bone work and implements of stone" (Maguire 1894:109). Nothing else is known about Maguire's foray into Nine Mile Canyon, including whether any of the sites he observed here contributed to Utah's exhibit at the World's Fair.

The Montgomery Years

Another Utah researcher—Henry Montgomery of the University of Deseret, which became the University of Utah in 1892—was actively investigating Utah's prehistoric sites in 1892, and in at least one instance Maguire and Montgomery worked on the same site at the same time. The list of sites Montgomery worked on is quite similar to the catalog of sites described in Maguire's brief report, and it is often assumed that Maguire and Montgomery were working together. But there is no mention in Maguire's report of Montgomery's assistance, nor does Montgomery's report mention that he was working with Maguire. In fact, a close reading of Montgomery's richly detailed descriptions reveals general disapproval for the methods being employed by Maguire.

> Preferring not to use the plough and scraper which were at the same time being freely used by the Territorial World's Fair representatives on the south side of this mound [Paragonah], I set to work, aided by five men employed for the purpose, to excavate and open up the remains of the ancient buildings. As is my custom, I carefully removed [the layers of prehistoric remains], inch by inch, with shovel, trowel and brush [Montgomery 1894:303].

Montgomery's attention to careful excavation reflected the changing attitudes of archaeological inquiry across the nation. His excavations were painstaking and methodical, and he reported his findings in a series of articles in Warren K. Moorehead's journal *The Archaeologist* (1894). In fact, Montgomery's descriptions of the ruins and rock art of Nine Mile Canyon constitute the first substantial attempt to describe the archaeology of northeastern Utah.

Like Maguire, Henry Montgomery was not native to Utah but, afflicted by professional wanderlust, found his way to Salt Lake City at age 41 after various teaching assignments in Canada and the United States. Born in Ontario, Canada, in 1849, he earned bachelor's and master's degrees in arts and sciences, first from the University of Toronto and later at Victoria University, also in Toronto, where he took courses in mathematics, mineralogy, geology, zoology, and paleontology. It is unknown if he studied archaeology, but his first known publication, an August 3, 1878, letter to the editor of the Toronto *Globe*, addressed "Indian remains in Simcoe and Muskoka," and he later wrote that he had been digging in prehistoric ossuaries in Canada since 1870. He studied many different disciplines and taught many subjects, ranging from the comparative anatomy and physiology of insects to Devonian rocks. After teaching briefly in Canada, he became a professor of natural sciences at (and vice president of) the University of North Dakota, where in 1883 he began excavating local burial mounds (Kapches 2003).

Henry Montgomery in the early 1890s. Photo used with permission of Special Collections, Marriott Library, University of Utah.

Montgomery left North Dakota in 1889, taught briefly in New York, and in July 1890 was hired by the University of Deseret, where he was appointed chief of mineralogy, geology, and natural history and curator of the Museum of Deseret University. During his tenure there, he published on topics ranging from mineral wax to the sands of the Great Salt Lake (Kapches 2003). But archaeology was Montgomery's lifelong passion, and Utah proved fertile ground to satisfy that yen.

In a series of three articles published in 1894, Montgomery offered rich accounts of relics recovered by collectors in San Juan County, of excavations he conducted at the foot of Mount Nebo near Nephi and at Paragonah, and of his investigations in Nine Mile Canyon. In passing, he mentioned he had also conducted investigations at Marysvale in Piute County, as well as in Beaver, Tooele, Salt Lake, Emery, Utah, Box Elder, Sevier, and Millard Counties, although he apparently never wrote about them.

Photographs from Montgomery's expedition into Nine Mile Canyon were later donated to the Royal Museum at the University of Toronto, and all are

Previously unpublished 1892 photograph taken in Nine Mile Canyon by the Henry Montgomery expedition. Photo used with permission of the Royal Ontario Museum, Canada (Copyright ROM).

dated "June 1892." The photographer who accompanied him is unknown, although it could have been "Sergeant P. Bartsch," described only as an assistant. Montgomery's account noted roughly 30 structural sites and 25 rock art sites located between the Sheep Canyon and Cottonwood Canyon tributaries (1894:336). It can be inferred that Montgomery also conducted excavations in Nine Mile Canyon from his comment, "From another house ruin the skeleton of a typical Cliff Dweller with flattened [cranium] was taken at a depth of five feet beneath the floor" (1894:340).

The wealth of artifacts present in 1892 was impressive, suggesting that the near absence of artifacts available to researchers today might be the result of more than a century of artifact collecting and looting. Montgomery described "considerable quantities of corn, shelled and unshelled, as well as gourds and water tanks" (1894:337); sandstone grinding stones of a different material than the natural sandstone of the area (1894:338); and corncobs, bison horn, painted pottery, and bone tools (1894:339).

Montgomery provided considerable architectural details, some of which, like the wooden construction beams that could furnish critical tree-ring dates, are no longer evident at open sites in Nine Mile Canyon. Among the architecture Montgomery described were three surface structures on top of a 50-foot-high "rock tower" with roofs constructed of heavy cedar logs laid horizontally and covered with heavy, flat stones. The logs and poles used in the construction of these structures "would make about a cord of wood, and they possessed distinct marks of the crude stone axes with which they had been cut into suitable lengths" (1894:338).

Although most of the report is clinical in its description, Montgomery also exhibited an occasional flair for the colorful.

> At three o'clock in the morning of a long and bright summer's day, my saddle-horse and that of my assistant stood at the door of the ranch house in readiness to carry us to the top of a peak some two miles distant, and upon which was a natural column of rock bearing prehistoric ruins. We soon mounted our steeds, forded the stream, and began the toilsome and dangerous ascent of the mountain, stopping to rest our sure-footed animals more and more frequently as we ascended. At length, after about three hours' continuous climbing, we reached a spot

Famous "bison" panel at Cottonwood Canyon. Photo by Ray Boren.

where we were obliged to abandon the horses and make the remainder of the trip on foot. In a short time we came to the rock column, which, although hard and solid, was much disintegrated, and had been vertically cleft and separated, leaving a dangerous gap between its two inclined and overhanging portions. By aid of cedar poles we succeeded in clambering to its summit, and there, in a situation that commanded a magnificent view of many canyons and hills, we found the ruins of four circular stone structures, which in my opinion, had once formed a lookout and signal military station [1894:340].

Taken in the context of the times, Montgomery's report offers minimal speculation. He did suggest the ancient peoples of Nine Mile Canyon and elsewhere in Utah, Arizona, and Colorado were "one and the same people," occupying the valleys and canyons at the same time, producing similar pottery, and raising food crops of similar kinds, "adapting themselves to the surrounding and changing conditions of nature" (1894:342).

More speculative was his assertion that "Utah, being on the outskirts of the country occupied by a great nation whose headquarters were probably in Mexico, might properly be expected to be provided with a considerable number of military posts or watch stations such as those herein described" (1894:340). Such conjectures were not that unusual at that time, and in many regards they are quite tame compared with the writings of his contemporaries.

No one knows what became of the artifacts described by Montgomery. It is possible that the materials, if turned over to the Columbian Exposition, were lost. At the conclusion of the World's Fair, the Utah exhibit was transported to San Francisco to the Midwinter Fair, where it was under the care of Don Maguire and Alonzo Young. When both men were summoned to return to Utah, the artifacts were left in the care of a "Mrs. Cain." According to the official report of the Utah World's Fair Commission, the Midwinter Fair was to have assumed all expenses to return the exhibit to Utah (see McDaniels 1894:111), but it is unknown if this was ever done.

The artifacts described by Montgomery may also have been included in the famous C. B. Lang Collection, which was the subject of considerable description in the first of Montgomery's three descriptive reports (1894). This collection was acquired by the Deseret Museum in Salt Lake City sometime before June 1894. It was later divided between the LDS Museum of Church History and Art in Salt Lake City and Brigham Young University in Provo. The portion acquired by BYU contained some materials collected by Montgomery, but the Nine Mile Canyon artifacts

ABOVE, A stone tower structure located near Petes Canyon in middle Nine Mile Canyon, 1892. Photo used with permission of the Royal Ontario Museum, Canada (Copyright ROM).

RIGHT, View of the same tower structure as in figure above in 2010. Photo courtesy of the Colorado Plateau Archaeological Alliance.

were not among the collection. Tragically, a considerable portion of the collection was subsequently misplaced or improperly catalogued, and the current location of most of the Montgomery artifacts is unknown (Phillips 1993:113). The recent discovery of the 1892 Nine Mile photographs at the Royal Ontario Museum has allowed archaeologists to begin reidentifying which sites Montgomery actually visited (see figures on p. 32).

Whether Montgomery and Maguire were working in partnership to bolster the Utah exhibit or in competition for collections, both men were motivated by insatiable personal curiosity. And collectively their efforts reflected the nascent interest of territorial officials in Utah's own archaeological riches—cultural treasures to be celebrated, respected, and shared with a national audience. The Utah exhibit was indeed a smashing success, earning the state international acclaim. According to the official report, an estimated two million people visited the exhibit, and "it is safe to say that no better opportunity could have been afforded in the way of advertising than by taking part in the Exposition" (McDaniels 1894:41).

Montgomery left the University of Utah in 1894 after being passed over for the Deseret Professorship of Geology in favor of James E. Talmage, a prominent Mormon scientist. He bounced from one teaching assignment to another, and in 1903 he completed his doctorate at Illinois Wesleyan University. His dissertation, titled *Prehistoric Man in the United States and Canada*, includes much of the same text as his articles in *The Archaeologist*. He became curator of the new museum at the University of Toronto, where he remained until he died suddenly during the 1918 flu epidemic. At that time, Montgomery's estate sold 50 cases of artifacts, notes, and books to the museum for $25. Among this collection were the Nine Mile Canyon photographs and a Nine Mile rock art image that he had pried from the canyon wall (Kapches 2003; Mima Kapches, personal communication 2010).

After the World's Fair

The flurry of interest, both public and professional, in the archaeological treasures of Nine Mile Canyon waned after the 1893 World's Fair. More than a decade passed before Byron Cummings of the University of Utah returned to the canyon in the summer of 1906 to initiate studies. But when he arrived, there was a

Nine Mile Canyon in the summer. Photo by Ray Boren.

confrontation with a party of Ute Indians who insisted that he leave the Nine Mile Canyon region immediately. In his firm but peaceful fashion, the Dean refused to turn around and go immediately, but insisted on staying overnight. In the course of these negotiations, he invited the Indians for supper. They accepted, and all ended happily, with the Dean leaving the next morning as he had promised [Willey 1988:4].

Cummings apparently paused long enough to collect two manos and a green granite groundstone tool. These items are currently catalogued at the Utah Natural History Museum in Salt Lake City. There is no indication that Cummings returned to Nine Mile Canyon. In 1909, J. Alden Mason also made a trip to the canyon, and photographs from that survey were made available to John Gillin during his 1936 excavations in upper

Nine Mile Canyon (in Gillin 1938:6). Mason, a recent graduate of the University of Pennsylvania, would receive a doctorate two years later from the University of California at Berkeley before going on to a stellar career as an anthropologist, linguist, and curator of the University Museum at the University of Pennsylvania. Mason spent 1909 working with renowned linguist Edward Sapir among the Uintah Utes, whose reservation is just north of Nine Mile Canyon (American Philosophical Society, John Alden Mason Papers, Background Note).

But neither Cummings nor Mason apparently wrote anything about visiting Nine Mile Canyon, nor did the canyon attract much attention from a cadre of archaeologists exploring elsewhere in northeastern Utah and northwestern Colorado between 1900 and 1925. In fact, when researchers from the Peabody Museum at Harvard University returned to Nine Mile Canyon in 1931, the area was still considered largely unknown and rich in scientific potential. And it would become fertile ground for a new generation of archaeologists who left their footprints here between 1928 and 1931: Noel Morss, Julian Steward, Donald Scott, and John Otis Brew.

3

Defining the Fremont Culture

Noel Morss, Harvard University, and the Claflin-Emerson Expedition

Bear in mind that I have never been a professional archaeologist....
Nor should I be addressed as "doctor."

—LETTER FROM NOEL MORSS TO J. ELDON DORMAN, 1980

Harvard University and Archaeology as Science

Henry Montgomery's titillating account in 1894 of spectacular ruins may have briefly thrust Nine Mile Canyon into the public spotlight, but serious academic interest in the canyon never materialized, and scarcely a mention of the canyon was made during the almost four decades that followed Montgomery's report. There was certainly no shortage of archaeological investigations under way in Utah during that period, and the University of Utah was actively engaged in stocking its new museum with exotic artifacts from San Juan County. So how did Nine Mile Canyon—one of the richest archaeological districts in the state—escape the attention of the state's archaeologists in the early twentieth century?

The dearth of inquiry can be explained, at least in part, by the scholarly interests of those who directed the nascent archaeology program at the University of Utah and their overriding preoccupation with artifact collections over scientific inquiry. Quite simply, the ruins of Nine Mile Canyon are comparatively small and the artifacts are frustratingly rare and unremarkable, at least when compared with the beacon call of the dramatic Ancestral Puebloan ruins and rich artifact discoveries of southeastern Utah. When presented with a choice between simple arrowheads and grinding stones from sites in Nine Mile Canyon or feather robes and painted pottery from San Juan County, it seems Dean Cummings and his protégés invariably chose the latter.

By 1930, however, a radical transformation in archaeological theory had occurred, mostly emanating from eastern research institutions but certainly influencing the University of Utah, which had just hired Julian Steward, a brilliant young scholar who had recently graduated from the University of California at Berkeley. For the first time, researchers trained as archaeologists embarked on expeditions with specific scientific questions. They took

OPPOSITE, Nine Mile Canyon petroglyph compositions feature dozens, sometimes hundreds, of strange and wonderful images. Photo by Ray Boren.

Spiral horned snake, Dry Canyon. Photo by Jerry D. Spangler.

detailed notes on everything from architectural characteristics to the stratigraphy of superimposed deposits, and they documented their observations with site maps, sketches, and photographs. And there was an expectation that every investigation would result in a published monograph.

It was within that burgeoning climate of scientific inquiry and exacting attention to detail that Nine Mile Canyon beckoned to a new generation of young archaeologists, not for the artifacts that could be collected but for the answers to intriguing questions surrounding the prehistoric peoples who occupied most of Utah north of the Colorado River. Were they merely the country cousins of the better-known Ancestral Puebloans? Were they a distinct culture unique to Utah? How were they different from the Puebloans? Noel Morss's classic 1931 treatise *Ancient Culture of the Fremont River in Utah* offered the first succinct definition of these peoples, and the moniker Fremont culture, used as early as 1928 (Morss 1928a, 1928b; see also Roberts 1929), has been engrained in the popular and professional literature ever since.

But Morss's perspectives, eloquently articulated in the monograph, were hardly unique. Rather, they were an amalgamation of ideas gleaned from years of association with his Harvard colleagues, in particular Donald Scott, but also John Otis Brew, Henry Roberts, and Alfred V. Kidder. Morss is lionized as the father of the Fremont culture concept. In reality, he was the first to articulate in a published manuscript what others had already surmised. And he made an argument so convincing that his publication preempted the need for a second monograph, to have been written by Roberts.

The Collectors

To understand how Nine Mile Canyon could be ignored for decades only to become the belle of the archaeological ball from 1928 to 1931 requires some historical perspective. In the early twentieth century, archaeology as a science simply did not exist. Those interested in antiquities were trained in other fields, sometimes in the natural sciences but sometimes not. They pursued their archaeological interests more as an appendage to their other teaching duties, often with a mandate from university officials to make collections of artifacts for their museums. Sites were excavated and in some cases destroyed for the artifacts they could produce (Hurst 1999).

This was certainly true at the University of Utah, which had a long-standing interest in the state's archaeology and sponsored a number of archaeological expeditions. In the early years of the twentieth century, this responsibility fell to Byron Cummings, who joined the university in 1893 as an instructor of Latin and English. He later became professor of ancient languages and, by 1915, the dean of the School of Arts and Sciences (he was also head of the newly created Archaeology Department). During the course of his 22-year tenure, Cummings started and directed the Archaeological and Historical Museum, and he enthusiastically embraced a university mandate to obtain a collection of Utah artifacts.

Cummings led periodic university expeditions to southeastern Utah beginning in 1907 and continuing through 1915, when he abruptly resigned in the midst of a campus-wide revolt over academic freedoms. Cummings briefly visited Nine Mile Canyon, but his emerging academic interest in archaeology was clearly focused on artifact-rich San Juan County and northern Arizona. As noted by Winston Hurst, "Unfortunately, Dr. Cummings' methods were well within the norm for the first decade of the twentieth century: His enthusiasm for artifact collection was not matched by an equal enthusiasm for data collection" (1999:2).

Among Cummings's students was Alfred V. Kidder, a visiting Harvard scholar who would later become one of the most eminent American archaeologists of the first half of the twentieth century, working under the auspices of the Peabody Museum at Harvard University. Kidder accompanied Cummings to White and Armstrong Canyons in 1907, and the colorful descriptions they wrote prompted President Theodore Roosevelt in 1908 to create Natural Bridges National Monument (Judd 1954:154). Kidder's passion was the prehistory of the Southwest, but he also had an abiding interest in the distant regions to the north of the Colorado River, at that time dubbed "the Northern Periphery." And in 1927, Kidder planted the seeds that would lead to a four-year expedition culminating in the first scientific investigations in Nine Mile Canyon.

Another of Cummings's students in 1912 and 1913 was Andrew Affleck Kerr, at the time a high school teacher from Ogden, Utah. In 1917, two

Cliff ruins in Nine Mile Canyon.
Photo by Jerry D. Spangler.

years after Cummings had left for the University of Arizona, Kerr enrolled in the graduate program in archaeology at Harvard University, presumably under the influence if not direct tutelage of Alfred V. Kidder. During his four years there earning his master's and doctoral degrees (with highest honors), he also held the position "In Charge of Summer Field Work for the University of Utah," although exactly what this entailed is not known (Hurst 1999). Kerr returned to the University of Utah in 1921, and in 1925 he was named head of the newly reorganized Anthropology Department.

There is no evidence that Nine Mile Canyon ever attracted Kerr's attention, which is probably a good thing. Although he was a nationally recognized scholar at the time (he had even been awarded Harvard's coveted Hemenway Fellowship), Kerr's legacy in Utah is a rather unsavory one: he initiated the practice of hiring local residents to dig into ancient ruins and middens to acquire collections for the university museum, a practice that encouraged the still prevalent illegal looting of archaeological sites for salable artifacts. As Hurst noted, "In fact, Kerr's field work had little to do with archaeology *per se* and everything to do with artifact collecting" (1999:5). This is no better illustrated than in a quotation attributed to him in a newspaper article kept by his descendants: "We want the biggest collection of Utah archeological specimens in the world right here in the state of Utah" (in Hurst 1999:5). If Kerr paid Nine Mile Canyon residents to recover local artifacts, there is no record of it, which is not surprising since Kerr never kept notes of any kind or published reports of his work.

A Passing Fancy

Kerr died suddenly of cancer in 1929, and his position was filled the next year by Julian Steward, a young rising star in the field of anthropology who eschewed the "artifacts" mentality of his predecessors, instead bringing an unprecedented attention to scientific detail. Steward had in 1929 received a doctorate in anthropology with a dissertation titled "The Ceremonial Buffoon of the American Indian: A Study of Ritualized Clowning and Role Reversals," after which he became the first anthropology lecturer at the University of Michigan (some biographical accounts credit him with starting the Anthropology Department there). But his intellectual passion was the indigenous Paiutes and Utes of the Great Basin, whom he'd studied since he was a teenager attending a small college in Nevada. He accepted the University of Utah position to be closer to his field of interest.

Steward was a prodigious writer and a keen observer who used his ethnographic skills to draw inferences from the archaeological record. In 1931, Steward visited the Uinta Basin to observe a Ute Sun Dance, but because of postponements he turned his attention to several prehistoric mounds along the Uinta River seven miles north of Fort Duchesne. His intent was to compare residential pithouses in the Uinta Basin with those he had earlier excavated in the Salt Lake Valley (1933:32; see also Allison 2010). Records at the Utah Natural History Museum indicate that Steward conducted excavations in Nine Mile Canyon, also in 1931, and that a variety of projectile points, maize remains, basketry, bones, and "dried lizards" were recovered. Steward did not specifically describe his Nine Mile Canyon investigations in his 1933 report or in his other publications, and the exact location of these investigations is not known.

However, archaeological evidence from the Uinta Basin and Nine Mile Canyon would make up a small portion of a later report in which Steward described a two-phase cultural sequence for Utah north of the Colorado River as "clearly derived from the Southwest, but does not correspond exactly to any of the cultural periods of the latter" (Steward 1940:468). Steward did not employ the term Fremont culture but rather described Phase I as a

culture consisting of a blend of Derived Basket Maker and Early Pueblo elements, which persisted with little change in the north.... It consisted of horticulture (maize, beans, squash) and several traits that were functionally dependent on it. At least a semi-sedentary life connected with farming warranted construction of a comparatively permanent lodge [1940:468–469; see also figure below].

Julian Steward's depiction of "earthen lodges" characteristic of northern Utah. Although he did not use the term "Fremont culture," these lodges are now recognized as typical Fremont pithouses. Illustration adapted from Steward's "Early Inhabitants of Western Utah" (1933). Image courtesy of the Utah Natural History Museum.

The cliffs of Nine Mile Canyon ascend like stairs to more than 1,000 feet above floodplain. Photo by Ray Boren.

Phase II was described as a migration of a "few people, at least, with posteriorly flattened, broad heads." Phase II villages were larger, and the population more dependent on horticulture. Houses of rectangular masonry rooms were built in clusters, typically along streams, and they had associated masonry granaries, although slab and jacal lodges continued to be used (1940:471).

With a personal scandal festering over his separation from his wife, educational psychologist Dorothy Nyswander, Steward left the University of Utah in 1935 for a position at the Smithsonian Institution, where he founded and directed the Institute for Social Anthropology. By 1946, he had become chairman of the Anthropology Department at Columbia University, then the most prestigious anthropology program in the United States. At the time of his death in 1972, he was recognized as one of the most influential anthropologists in the nation's history.

During his short tenure in Utah, he was clearly intrigued by Nine Mile Canyon, although the exact nature of his work there remains tantalizingly elusive. Today we are left with only passing references such as "the slab

Peabody Museum crews accessing granary on narrow ledge in Range Creek Canyon, 1931. Photo (98470075) used with permission of the Peabody Museum of Archaeology and Ethnology, Harvard University.

houses in Nine Mile Canyon south of the Uintah Basin appear to have a close relationship to Basketmaker slab houses of southern Utah" (1940:469). It is possible that Steward's Nine Mile Canyon field notes are among those that have recently been discovered at the University of Illinois. The vacancy left by Steward's departure from the University of Utah opened the door to another rising young scholar, John P. Gillin, who, like Steward, was an anthropologist first and foremost.

The Claflin-Emerson Expedition

There is a reason why archaeologists rarely ventured into southern Utah's canyon country: the waterless region can be near impassable without seasoned guides, and the deserts are desolate and formidable. Places like the Kaiparowits Plateau and Waterpocket Fold and, farther north, the Tavaputs Plateau remain largely wilderness even today, laughing at the hubris of modern folly that they can be tamed. This forbidding terrain makes the saga of the Claflin-Emerson Expedition into the region all the more remarkable. Imagine young Harvard University students, none of whom were accustomed to the saddle and none hardened to the rigors of western cowboy life, venturing into an unknown wilderness in pursuit of rumors and whispers of ancient ruins. They were accompanied only by local wranglers and a photographer. Inexperience notwithstanding, they were fearless when it came to traversing narrow cliff ledges, exploring many sites that are simply not accessible today without considerable risk to life and limb. But they survived in the wilderness with nary a scratch, leaving behind in the vaults at the Peabody Museum at Harvard a wealth of detailed journals, sketches, and photographs.

The Claflin-Emerson Expedition was inspired by Alfred V. Kidder, who in 1927 was curator of Southwestern Archaeology at the Peabody Museum. He suggested to William H. Claflin Jr. and Raymond Emerson that they take a pack trip through portions of southern Utah north and west of the Colorado River, an area virtually unknown to archaeologists at the time. Claflin, Emerson, and their spouses soon embarked on a wide-ranging trip through southern Utah and at once recognized the region's archaeological importance. On their return to Harvard, they agreed to fund an extended reconnaissance to be carried out by the Peabody Museum, where

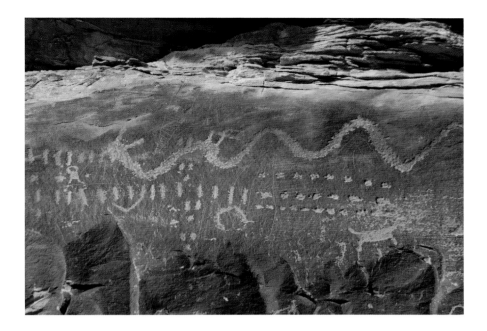

Horned snake, Nine Mile Canyon. Photo by Ray Boren.

Claflin was curator of Southeastern Archaeology (Gunnerson 1969; see also Donald Scott Collection, Peabody Museum).

Fieldwork in 1928 and 1931 was directed by Donald Scott, at the time assistant director of the museum, and in 1929 and 1930 by Henry B. Roberts, himself a rising star in the field of archaeology. Over a four-year period, the survey extended from the Kaiparowits Plateau on the west and south, to the Moab and Monticello areas on the east, and to the Uinta Basin on the north. The Claflin-Emerson Expedition was not the only research foray into the northern Colorado Plateau at that time, but it was certainly the most prestigious and the most ambitious in scope.

Ironically, it was not the work of Donald Scott and Henry Roberts that would have the greatest impact on Utah archaeology. Rather, it was a manuscript drafted in 1928 by expedition participant Noel Morss (1928a, 1928b; published by the Peabody Museum in 1931) that would forever influence archaeological theory north of the Colorado River (Brew 1982). The monograph, published using Morss's personal funds, effectively defined the Fremont culture, a term still used by archaeologists today to describe farmers and foragers north of the Colorado River.

A second major monograph, by Henry B. Roberts, was to have incorporated the observations made by crews under the direction of Scott and Roberts. However, Roberts left the Peabody Museum in the summer of 1930 to assume responsibilities with the Carnegie Institution, and subsequent illness forced him to abandon the monograph. James Gunnerson later published many of the Claflin-Emerson Expedition notes in his

Donald Scott, director of the Peabody Museum from 1932 to 1948. Photo (2004.24.26810A) used with permission of the Peabody Museum of Archaeology and Ethnology, Harvard University.

synthesis of the Fremont culture (1969), but for unknown reasons large portions of the expedition field notes were not included in this work, and dozens of sites described in the journals were omitted. Morss's journals from 1928 and 1929 have been lost, although two 1928 summary reports (Morss 1928a, 1928b) are archived at the Peabody Museum and could reflect close transcriptions of his 1928 journal. Likewise, any draft report initiated by Roberts is also missing from the Peabody Museum collections, although the museum has his detailed journals.

Uncommon Genius

The story of the Claflin-Emerson Expedition would be incomplete without the remarkable happenstance of Noel Morss. It has been stated authoritatively in numerous publications that Morss was an expedition participant in 1928 and 1929, and indeed he was, to a point. He was not an archaeologist with impressive credentials. He was not an archaeology student preparing for a grand career studying world cultures. He was not even trained in archaeological theories and methods. He was a remarkably intelligent man with a deep and abiding interest in archaeology who happened to tag along on the Utah expeditions.

Years later, Morss wrote to J. Eldon Dorman at the College of Eastern Utah that he felt like a fraud in archaeological contexts because his law degree was not an "honest-to-goodness" doctorate. "Bear in mind that I have never been a professional archaeologist.... Nor should I be addressed as 'doctor'" (Morss 1980). Self-deprecation aside, his keen intellect was unequivocally respected by the Peabody Museum hierarchy. In November 1930, when Donald Scott convened an informal meeting of the top archaeological minds in the country—Kidder, Frank Roberts, Henry Roberts, Edgar Howard, and Samuel J. Guernsey—to address "necessary objectives and refinements of methodology" surrounding southwestern ceramics, Noel Morss was invited to participate, even though he was only 26 years old at the time and practicing law, not archaeology. The Peabody Museum's esteem for Morss persisted through the remainder of his life. In 1954, he was appointed chairman of the Visiting Committee, Harvard University Department of Anthropology and the Peabody Museum, and from 1955 to 1960 he was a Peabody Museum Research Fellow in Prehistory of the

Pete's Village site. Photo by Ray Boren.

American Southwest (see biographical note to the Noel Morss Papers, Harvard University Library).

Born in 1904, Morss grew up in Chestnut Hills, a well-heeled suburb of Boston, where his neighbors happened to be Thalassa Cruso, often described as the "Julia Child of horticulture," and Hugh O'Neill Hencken, a famed Old World archaeologist and curator of European archaeology at the Peabody Museum. Hencken cultivated Morss's interest in archaeology, introducing him to Alfred Kidder, who took a liking to the young man. He accompanied a museum expedition to northern Arizona in 1925, and two years later Morss himself led a museum-sponsored expedition to the same area—much to the chagrin of Byron Cummings, at that time with the University of Arizona, who claimed the region as his own "bailiwick" (Morss 1960).

As Morss wrote in a May 17, 1960, letter to Otis Marston, Kidder had asked Morss to investigate the Navajo Canyon country. Cummings got wind of the plan and wrote the director of the Peabody Museum to object to Morss's expedition. The director "first forbade me to go, later grudgingly giving permission on condition that we did no excavating. Later Kidder told me to disregard this restriction and we did do some digging, for which [the director] never quite forgave me."

This incident occurred a year after Morss had received his undergraduate degree in economics from Harvard University, in 1926. He later graduated from Harvard Law School in 1929. Harvard Law has never been an easy task, but somehow Morss did it while juggling archaeological

Noel Morss's crews excavating at Fish Creek Cove near Grover, Utah, in 1928. This site provided the bulk of Morss's monograph defining the Fremont culture. Photo used with permission of the Peabody Museum of Archaeology and Ethnology, Harvard University.

expeditions to Arizona in 1927 and Utah in 1928 and 1929. And he still found time to write two monographs, one on his Navajo Canyon investigations, titled *Notes on the Archaeology of the Kaibito and Rainbow Plateaus in Arizona: Report on the Explorations, 1927*, and the other on the Fremont culture, both published in 1931.

It is not clear from the correspondence on file with the Peabody Museum why Kidder would entrust the Arizona expedition to a first-year law student or what qualified Morss to engage in scientifically controlled excavations. Judging from photographs of Morss's 1928 excavations at Fish Creek Cove near the Fremont River, his technique involved massive pits and lots of them. A close reading of *Ancient Culture of the Fremont River* reveals serious attention to detail (Morss 1931a), whereas the photographs suggest the excavations were anything but methodical (but perhaps not unusual for the day).

By the spring of 1928, the Peabody Museum was preparing to launch the four-year Claflin-Emerson Expedition to explore unknown regions of Utah north of the Colorado River. How Morss came to participate is not known, although we can surmise that it resulted from his close relationship with his patrons, Hencken and Kidder. Once the expedition reached Utah, it split into two groups, one led by Donald Scott and bolstered by Harvard University students, and the other led by Morss, whose crew consisted of himself and some local residents, including a local relic collector named Clarence Mulford, who had previously looted the sites but agreed to guide Morss to them. Morss and Mulford remained friends for years afterward.

Based on correspondence in the Peabody Museum archives, there was apparently little communication between Morss and expedition leader Scott, nor was there prior planning as to which group would investigate which areas. The end result was considerable overlap in the surveyed areas, with the Scott-led group coming across and documenting sites already visited, and in some cases excavated, by Morss. Whether or not there was hostility between Morss and Scott is not known, but the two men exchanged terse letters during 1929 and 1930 during the preparation of Morss's monograph (Scott was the editor of the monograph), followed by letters of apology and conciliation.

The fact that Morss operated independently and without oversight from the more experienced Scott suggests a couple of possible scenarios: that Morss was recognized as a highly qualified field archaeologist and the expedition could maximize its efforts by having two crews in the field simultaneously, or that Morss was dispatched to "do his own thing" to keep himself amused and his powerful patrons at bay while the others did the serious work of real archaeology.

With the foundation already laid for a monograph after completion of the 1928 field season, Morss returned to the Fremont River area in 1929 with Lyon Boston to reexamine a few sites and investigate some new sites in the Waterpocket Fold area, where they left their names etched on an alcove wall. And for reasons not entirely clear, the men then made an arduous trip more than 100 miles to the north to Nine Mile Canyon. Morss's observations were confined to a 10-mile section of Nine Mile Canyon between the Preston Nutter Ranch and Cottonwood Canyon, where he noted an abundance of dry-laid stone masonry but did not assign any great antiquity to the structures. Until a short time before his arrival, Nine Mile Canyon "had been part of the Ute reservation," and he wrote that the "numerous low walls of rocks without mortar in small shelters and on points on the cliffs are attributable to them" (Morss 1931a:28; author's note: Nine Mile Canyon was never part of the Ute reservation).

Morss described only three sites in Nine Mile Canyon, all rockshelter or cave sites. His Nine Mile Canyon investigations included the excavation of a partially mummified body of a child in Rasmussen Cave. It lay on its back, the arms flexed at the sides and the femurs pointed almost straight up, the lower legs missing. The lower jaw was also missing, and the skull

Noel Morss and Lyon Boston inscribed their names in an alcove in the Waterpocket Fold area, 1929. Photo courtesy of Craig Harmon, Bureau of Land Management, Richfield District.

showed moderate occipital deformation. There was no evidence of anything accompanying the burial other than rotted fragments of mountain sheep skin adhering to the back of the head (Morss 1931a:29).

Morss also devoted some attention to Nine Mile Canyon rock art, describing a variety of styles that "contrast with the comparative uniformity" of Fremont rock art in other areas (1931a:42). He believed the Fremont anthropomorphs developed from Basketmaker prototypes and indicated the personification of supernatural beings in forms similar to those in the Southwest. Morss argued that "on the whole" the rock art of Nine Mile Canyon showed more resemblance to that of the Pueblo area than to the Fremont region proper (1931a:40), the exception being the large painted figures in and near Rasmussen Cave, which are more representative of "a culture similar to, if not indistinguishable from, that of the Fremont valley" (1931a:41).

Morss published his findings in 1931 before the crews led by Scott had even embarked on their final field season, which would take them to Nine Mile Canyon. How the manuscript came to be published so quickly is a testament to Morss's determination to produce the monograph. Quite simply, the Peabody Museum, at the time suffering the ill effects of the Great Depression, had no funds to publish anything. So the well-to-do Morss simply wrote out checks to the museum for $1,850 to publish both the northern Arizona and the Fremont River manuscripts—the first published by the museum in years (see Scott 1931b, 1931c).

Morss's Nine Mile Canyon observations played only a minor role in the overall monograph, and the canyon does not feature prominently in his proposed Fremont culture, which he described as "partly and perhaps predominantly agricultural." He continued:

> The inhabitants of the Fremont region were also dependent in good part on the game supply. Small granaries apart from any dwellings show that the people moved about, in all probability living in flats in the summer and cultivating corn, and in the winter in sheltering canyons around the mountains and devoting themselves to hunting. In its general features, the culture remained at the Basketmaker III level, as shown by the pottery, the figurines, the absence of cotton and turkeys, the twined-woven mats, the fur cloth, the relative abundance of coiled basketry, the various forms of snares and traps, and the general shape of the anthropomorphic pictographs. Only in a few characteristics— the bow and arrow, mountain sheep pictographs, stone drills and possibly head deformation—does the culture show traits in common with the early Pueblo culture with which it had contacts [1931a:76–77].

It is a definition that modern archaeologists find remarkably valid eight decades later.

Into the Tavaputs

As Morss's monograph was being prepared for publication in 1931, Donald Scott assumed the leadership of the final year's reconnaissance into the unknown Tavaputs Plateau and later into the better-known Uinta Basin. Among the participants that final year were Alfred Kidder's son, A. V. Kidder II, and John "Jo" Brew, who later rose to prominence in the wake of landmark research at Alkali Ridge near Monticello, Utah. Also participating were three young students named William Bowers, Waldo Forbes,

Alfred V. Kidder II, the son of the famed southwestern archaeologist, focused his attention on Nine Mile Canyon in 1931. Photo (122520040) used with permission of the Peabody Museum of Archaeology and Ethnology, Harvard University.

ABOVE, John Otis Brew, known for his work at Alkali Ridge in southeastern Utah in 1932, the year after he worked in Nine Mile Canyon. Photo (95500097) used with permission of the Peabody Museum of Archaeology and Ethnology, Harvard University.

RIGHT, The Claflin-Emerson Expedition, in lower Gray Canyon, prepares to trek into the East Tavaputs Plateau, 1931. Photo (9458007) used with permission of the Peabody Museum of Archaeology and Ethnology, Harvard University.

and James Dennison. Accompanying the archaeologists were local guides, including celebrated Utah guide and photographer David Rust (see Swanson 2007), although these ancillary figures are rarely mentioned by name in the journals and it is unclear who accompanied the exploring parties at different points.

For its final field season, the Claflin-Emerson Expedition left Green River, Utah, in early July 1931, proceeding on horseback north up the east bank of the Green River and across the East Tavaputs Plateau through Grand and Uintah Counties. The expedition spent considerable time visiting, describing, and digging into masonry ruins in the Hill Creek and Willow Creek areas before crossing the Green River on a ferry owned at the time by Chuck Sands just north of Nine Mile Creek, although the group mistakenly called it the Muse Ferry after one of the employees (Scott 1931a:6). The expedition established a base camp at the Pace Ranch in lower Nine Mile Canyon, and after an unspecified amount of time exploring and documenting archaeological sites in lower Nine Mile Canyon, the crew split into three small groups. The first group continued surveys in the middle portion of Nine Mile Canyon, and the second explored the upper reaches of Nine Mile Canyon.

The third group, consisting of Bowers, Dennison, and Forbes, was dispatched with horses and mules to conduct a two-week reconnaissance of drainages to the south and east of Nine Mile Canyon, including Range Creek, where there were at least two remote ranches, one operated by cattle baron Preston Nutter and the other a small ranch operated by Italian

immigrant John Darioli, where the crew bivouacked for several days. The expedition described at least 29 sites in the Range Creek drainage (Scott 1931a:7; see also Spangler, Barlow, and Metcalfe 2004).

The expedition then proceeded north along the west bank of the Green River, where they became the first archaeologists to venture into Desolation Canyon. They explored several small side canyons, including Trail, Three, Snap, and Rock Creek. They then turned westward up Steer Ridge to the headwaters of Flat Canyon, then east down Jack Canyon back to the Green River, north along the Green River, and back to the Pace

ABOVE, Described by the Claflin-Emerson Expedition in 1931, this granary above the Pace Ranch is perhaps the largest yet documented in Nine Mile Canyon. Photo by Jerry D. Spangler.

RIGHT, Nordell's Fort, near the Pace Ranch, the base camp of the Claflin-Emerson Expedition during its foray into Nine Mile Canyon. Photo by Jerry D. Spangler.

Ranch through Rock House Canyon (Dennison 1931; Forbes 1931; Bowers 1931; see also typewritten transcripts of all 1931 notes, cited here as Scott 1931a), a distance of more than 100 miles in some of the harshest canyon environments imaginable. At least 20 sites were described in Desolation Canyon, all characterized as continuing the same types of rock art as found in Nine Mile Canyon, as well as an abundance of adobe granaries with jacal roofs (Scott 1931a:10).

While Dennison, Forbes, and Bowers were off exploring, Scott, Brew, and Kidder were busy documenting sites in Nine Mile Canyon. Thirty-four architectural and cave sites, as well as dozens of rock art sites, were described in Nine Mile Canyon, including Nordell's Fort, perhaps the best-preserved example of a prehistoric tower or "fort" remaining in the canyon, and a massive two-story granary above the Pace Ranch itself. They were especially impressed with what they called PR4-25, located at the mouth of Devil's Canyon and described as a "veritable prehistoric apartment house" situated 300 hundred feet above the valley floor with sheer drops on the Nine Mile Canyon side. The site was shielded by a defensive wall with a doorway and a series of narrow ledges on which were "unquestionable living sites." Above these ledges were granaries. On the top of the butte and on two different levels were groups of rooms. Storage cists of upright slabs were located under various overhangs. And on top of the boulder, crowning the whole, was a perfectly round "fort" (Scott 1931a:57–61). There is little remaining of this site today.

More significant, however, were the excavations they undertook at Rasmussen Cave, a site that had been dug two years before by Morss and

View of the doorway controlling access to PR4-25, a series of structures across a pinnacle top near Devil's Canyon. The site has yet to be formally documented to modern standards. Photo by Jerry D. Spangler.

earlier that year by looters. At least two and possibly four burials had been removed before Scott arrived here. At the bottom of a "refuse heap," Scott's crews unearthed yet another skeleton, this one without cranial deformation and with small amounts of soft tissue adhering to it. The remains were located in direct association with possible spear blades and an atlatl, complete with foreshafts and attached stone points. The individual was wearing moccasins of a type different from later Fremont moccasins. Moccasins also had been placed over the head, and buckskin leggings and an extra moccasin tied with a piece of cedar bark were located beneath the head. "It was probably a medicine bundle, since it contained red paint pigment in a small buckskin pouch, a serrated stone artifact, a hafted blade, the wooden portions of four foreshafts and a piece of worked horn" (Gunnerson 1969:101). Also associated with the burial were a flint drill, five chipped blades, a skin bag, a bone awl, a hafted flaker, a piece of fur cloth, and miscellaneous pieces of cordage.

The descriptive preoccupation with what is now commonly labeled a Basketmaker burial has led to a perception that Rasmussen Cave was occupied before the advent of ceramics. But a closer reading of the participant journals reveals that the site was exceptionally complex with evidence of multiple occupations, presumably over a long period of time. Portions of the cave had few if any ceramics. Other areas had ceramics and unfired clay figurines. Noel Morss later wrote Brew seeking clarification on the association of the figurines with the Basketmaker burial, to which Brew replied in a February 15, 1932, letter, "possibly the figurines belonged to a period intermediate in time between Basket-Maker 2 and the particular pottery-using people, the evidence of whom was found in the hard earth portion of the cave. Potsherds were not actually abundant in the latter section, but they were much more so than in any other site we encountered on the Tavaputs Plateau" (Brew 1932).

Rasmussen Cave remains the only site excavated in Nine Mile Canyon with evidence of Archaic or Basketmaker antecedents to the Fremont. As such, it is one of the most significant sites in the canyon.

Scott later synthesized the field notes from 1931, offering his own observations of Nine Mile Canyon's unique archaeology. But these notes were not published, probably due to the primacy of Morss's monograph as well as Roberts's illness, and they remained largely forgotten in the Peabody Museum basement until James Gunnerson published portions of them in 1969. Scott's observations are particularly relevant to Nine Mile Canyon. He noted that the dry-laid masonry west of the Green River was of considerably better quality than that observed in Hill Creek Canyon east of the Green River. Although similar in construction style, the West Tavaputs architecture featured multiple courses of more carefully laid sandstone slabs. Despite the differences, Scott determined that the sites were essentially the same (1931a:6).

> The houses differ greatly from any previously encountered in that the stone walls are not and do not seem to have been very high. They are never of more than two or three courses and furthermore there is not a sufficient number of stones lying about to support a supposition of original greater height. Evidently some sort of perishable construction was built up from a base consisting of a low stone wall [1931a:7–8].

Typical Nine Mile granary. Photo by Jerry D. Spangler.

A considerable number of granaries were observed throughout the West Tavaputs Plateau, which presumed a large prehistoric population. In an attempt to prove that hypothesis, Scott directed efforts to the flat or slightly sloping bench areas just above the valley floor, most jutting from the south canyon wall, where open dwelling sites were recorded, predominantly circular rooms. Sometimes a "fort" or a defensive wall was constructed at the point of access (1931a:7–8). Like Montgomery (1894:340–342), Reagan (1931h:8), and later Gillin (1938:22–32), Scott and the other crew members were struck by the defensive orientation of the surface structures, most of them located on pinnacles and rock outcrops a good distance above the valley floor (Scott 1931a; see also Brew 1931; Kidder 1931).

The expedition also recorded and photographed dozens of rock art sites in the region. In fact, Nine Mile Canyon was described as "almost a continuous picture gallery" (Scott 1931a:10). Scott was enamored of Utah rock art, and over the course of the next 35 years accumulated thousands of photographs and sketches, the last ones added to his collection only a few days before his death in 1967 (Brew, in Schaafsma 1971:xvii–xix). Scott, who became director

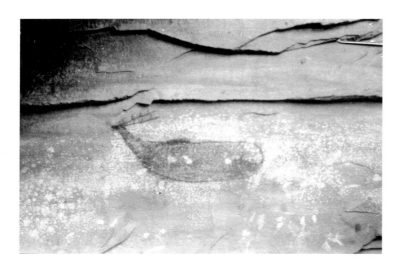 

of the Peabody Museum in 1932, promised the photographs would "be analyzed in the near future" (Scott 1931a:5), but that report was never written.

A Legacy Revisited

The Claflin-Emerson Expedition remains a hallmark of archaeological inquiry. It was the first major exploration of the most remote regions of Utah north of the Colorado River. It resulted in a definition of the Fremont culture that remains largely intact. It established the archaeological importance of the northern Colorado Plateau, something that successive generations of researchers—Julian Steward, John Gillin, Jesse Jennings, and others—would build on in the years to come. But despite its significance, this legacy was neglected. The expedition field notes were not published in a timely manner and were largely forgotten in the Peabody Museum archives. And for reasons not entirely clear, James Gunnerson, who examined the notes as part of his doctoral dissertation at Harvard University, published only a portion of them (Gunnerson 1969). Until recently, the location of the sites they described in the Nine Mile Canyon area and elsewhere on the West Tavaputs Plateau remained unknown.

In 2003, the Colorado Plateau Archaeological Alliance (CPAA) embarked on a multiyear project to reidentify and thoroughly document the expedition's 1931 sites. Working closely with the Peabody Museum, and with the help of generous grants from the Utah Division of State History and the National Park Service, CPAA has now identified almost 70 Claflin-Emerson Expedition sites in the region, including almost all the sites visited in Range Creek (Spangler, Barlow, and Metcalfe 2004) and Desolation

Canyon (Spangler and Jones 2009). The effort is now focused on Nine Mile Canyon, where as of 2012, about 20 sites have been reidentified.

Why is this important? By comparing historic photographs taken in 1931 (and later) with a site's current condition, researchers can evaluate the rate of site degradation over time. They can begin to understand which sites are at risk to vandals and looters, and they can even estimate when past looting might have occurred. And in some instances they can glean important information about a site that has since been largely destroyed. These efforts can then help land managers and private property owners protect the canyon's rich archaeological legacy for future generations.

LEFT, Same masonry structure as in figure at right, as it appeared in 2007 when it was redocumented by CPAA. Photo courtesy of the Colorado Plateau Archaeological Alliance, Ogden, Utah.

RIGHT, View of a masonry structure in the Peter's Point area of Desolation Canyon as it appeared in 1931. Photo (985770058) used with permission of the Peabody Museum of Archaeology and Ethnology, Harvard University.

4

On the Fringe of Science
Albert Reagan and the Para-archaeologists

The concept of the Great Plumed Serpent in Utah seems farfetched, but were the same figure sculptured in Mexico or Yucatan, all doubt of such intent would be removed. —FRANK BECKWITH, 1932

Amateurs or Professionals? Archaeology Outside Academia

The collective work of Julian Steward, Donald Scott, and Noel Morss clearly marked the genesis of serious scientific inquiry in Nine Mile Canyon. But by no means did they have a monopoly on Nine Mile Canyon research. The 1930s also marked the emergence of the para-archaeologists, or pseudo-archaeologists—enthusiastic and often accomplished individuals who professed an adherence to the archaeological methods of the day but who were largely untrained in careful excavation techniques. Unfettered by the higher academic standards of their university counterparts, they sometimes speculated wildly on the origins of prehistoric cultures in the region. And they were particularly enamored of the Nine Mile rock art, something their more esteemed academic colleagues eschewed as largely irrelevant. In many respects, these men (they were all men) were responsible for bringing Nine Mile Canyon and its myriad rock art sites to the attention of a national audience through scores of colorful accounts published in natural history journals.

The history of archaeological research in Nine Mile Canyon would be woefully incomplete without the contributions of three individuals in particular: Frank Beckwith, a Utah newspaper publisher and an accomplished photographer; Albert Reagan, a Stanford-educated teacher with the U.S. Indian Field Service; and Alfred E. Gaumer, whose written accounts offer remarkable attention to scientific detail that suggests at least some level of formal training. Reagan, who held a doctorate in geology, was taken seriously by some of his archaeologist contemporaries, and he was eventually awarded a professorship at Brigham Young University, the first "anthropology professor" at that institution (Allison 2010). Beckwith's legacy was in large part destroyed. And Gaumer has all but been ignored and forgotten.

OPPOSITE, "The Juggler" is a popular tourist attraction in Nine Mile Canyon. Photo by Ray Boren.

The Beckwith Legacy

An enthusiastic describer of Utah rock art, Frank Beckwith was an amateur archaeologist and newspaper publisher from Delta, Utah, who spent much of the 1920s and 1930s photographing Utah rock art and making descriptive reports for *El Palacio*, the journal of the Museum of New Mexico. Though Beckwith's later interpretations were purely speculative, of more objective value are the 300 photographs he claimed to have taken in the Clear Creek area near Richfield and in Nine Mile Canyon. A high-quality photograph of a rock art panel depicting long-legged waterbirds at the mouth of Currant Canyon, a northern tributary to Nine Mile Canyon, graced the cover of the October 1932 issue of *El Palacio*. Portions of Beckwith's photo collection were located in the possession of his granddaughter, Sue Dutson, who indicated that an undetermined number of original photographs were destroyed before his death. Other photographs were found recently in the possession of the Peabody Museum at Harvard University.

Beckwith first visited Nine Mile Canyon in June 1931, at least a month before the arrival of Donald Scott and the Claflin-Emerson Expedition, and he was immediately struck by similarities between rock art there and what he had previously photographed in Clear Creek Canyon some 130 miles to the southwest. He also observed that Nine Mile Canyon rock art featured three elements not found in Clear Creek Canyon: horned serpents, bison, and well-executed birds. He noted, for example, "I had seen in Clear Creek Canyon a poorly executed bird, and a turkey gobbler, but not such a near-peacock form as this one presented" (1931:219). He was also enamored of the abundant horned-snake figures, which became the subject of a second report, in which he observed, "The concept of the Great Plumed Serpent in Utah seems farfetched, but were the same figure sculptured in Mexico or Yucatan, all doubt of such intent would be removed" (1932:147).

The Necklace Mystery

Beckwith mentioned that two weeks before he arrived in Nine Mile Canyon a "party had dug in a cave at the Rasmussen property, and found

Frank Beckwith, a newspaper publisher from Delta, Utah, was one of the most prolific photographers of Utah archaeology of his day. Photo courtesy of the Beckwith family, Delta, Utah.

The Sandhill Crane Panel at the mouth of Currant Canyon was featured on the cover of *El Palacio* in 1932. Photo by Ray Boren.

a tiny mummy which was resting upon a coarsely woven mat of cedar bark" (1931:220). This is clearly a reference to the large alcove referred to as Rasmussen Cave today. Beckwith did not see the mummy, but he was told "on good authority" it was only 22 inches long, yet the skull and fully developed teeth were those of an adult. He also described other artifacts recovered by the amateur excavators at the cave, including a woven bag, two moccasins, a corncob on a broken metate, two woven baskets (one with an arrow foreshaft inside), a needle, and fragments of cloth. "A most

Rock art at Rasmussen Cave.
Photo by Ray Boren.

wonderful find" was a necklace 11 feet long, consisting of 2,750 cut-to-size, bored, and polished stones of a shiny black, varied with a thin, shell-like white bone (1931:221).

Beckwith's account is supported by Albert Reagan (1931j). Reagan identified the diggers as Lee Snyder and E. S. Noe, of nearby Myton, Utah. Reagan augmented the list of artifacts removed from Rasmussen Cave to include two human scalps, black obsidian, a snowshoe frame, knife blades eight inches long, a possible dog skeleton "the size of a Norway rat," a piece of sandstone that had been used as a paint palette, and two additional human skeletons (1933a:57–58). Reagan indicated that the collection was exhibited at rodeos throughout the Pacific Northwest until the owners divided it in half. The necklace? Also cut in half. The whereabouts of the collection was unknown as of 1933 (Reagan 1933a:57).

Indeed, the artifacts removed from Rasmussen Cave in the late spring of 1931 constitute perhaps the most spectacular cache ever recovered from Nine Mile Canyon. But the cache, the necklace in particular, also conjures a perplexing mystery, not because of what Beckwith and Reagan wrote but because of the descriptions of a third party. In two richly detailed reports in *The Masterkey*, the journal of the Southwest Museum in Los Angeles, Alfred E. Gaumer—we don't know who he was or if he represented a research institution—wrote that he conducted excavations at a cave site in August 1934. Among the items he mentions were a "puppy" associated with the burial of a child and, at the head of another burial, "a string of beads composed of slate and white bone, with a single bead of red stone.

Nine Mile Creek in the fall.
Photo by Ray Boren.

Irregularly strung, the beads lay in eight coils, with the original sinew string in place, and measuring 11 feet in length. There were 2,771 beads altogether, representing an incredible amount of work and lapidarian skill, and a fine example of ancient pre-Pueblo Art" (Gaumer 1937:165).

Nowhere in Gaumer's two reports does he mention Nine Mile Canyon or Rasmussen Cave by name. In fact, Gaumer leads the reader to believe the cave is located in Desolation Canyon along the Green River. But what are the chances that two virtually identical necklaces, both 11 feet long and both with almost the same number of beads, would be recovered from the same general area at roughly the same time? And how much more unlikely is it that both sites would have contained the remains of a very small dog associated with the burial of a child?

After a careful reading of the Gaumer reports, I believe, though I cannot prove, that Gaumer was actually a participant in the June 1931 amateur expedition to Rasmussen Cave that might have included at least two local men from Myton. Both reports may have been belated attempts by Gaumer to apologize and atone for the fact the expedition evolved into

This rock art site near Desborough Canyon, a tributary of Nine Mile Canyon, is depicted in Gaumer's 1937 account of his cave excavations, which were probably at Rasmussen Cave. Photo by Steven J. Manning.

nothing more than a scavenger hunt for exotic artifacts. But rather than accept responsibility for the egregious lapse in judgment, he obscured the location of the cave sites and modified the year he dug there to make it appear that it occurred after the "discovery" already published in reports by both Reagan and Beckwith. Here's my case:

- Beckwith and Reagan never saw the collection, but rather were told about it, and hence their catalog of artifacts would undoubtedly differ from that described by Gaumer, who was there. But several items appear in Gaumer's list of artifacts that are also mentioned by Reagan or Beckwith. Of course, there is the puppy associated with a child burial and the necklace. Beckwith also mentions that two baskets were recovered; Gaumer describes two baskets in great detail. Beckwith mentions that one basket contained an arrow fore-shaft; Gaumer says one basket contained "a complete set of flaking tools." Reagan mentions knife blades; Gaumer describes complete atlatl dart points. Beckwith mentions a "tiny mummy" resting on a coarsely woven mat of cedar bark; Gaumer describes an individual about 12 years old resting on a matting of juniper bark.

- Gaumer was unequivocally in Nine Mile Canyon in the 1930s: the 1937 report contains one photograph of a rock art site near Desborough Canyon, east of Rasmussen Cave, and another photo of a rock art site near Gate Canyon, west of Rasmussen Cave. Suspiciously, Gaumer never once mentioned that he had been in

Nine Mile Canyon, even though the canyon was well known at the time of his reports.

- The 1937 report also contains a photograph of the "puppy." It is consistent with Reagan's description of a dog the size of a large rat.

- It is important to distinguish what Gaumer describes in the 1937 report from the descriptions in his 1939 report. The 1937 report, which describes the necklace, puppy, and baskets—and includes the two photographs of rock art sites in Nine Mile Canyon—is probably an account of his excavations at Rasmussen Cave. Nowhere in that report does he offer sufficient clues as to the cave's location, only that it was in the area of Desolation Canyon. The 1939 report describes a different cave site (Gaumer calls it Big Wash Cave), and the only clue he offers regarding location is that he had spent a month investigating small caves and rockshelters in the West Tavaputs Plateau area, again an overly broad description. The infant strapped to a cradle board, the subject of the 1939 report, is not

This rock art site near Gate Canyon, a tributary of Nine Mile Canyon, is depicted in Gaumer's 1937 account of his cave excavations, which were probably at Rasmussen Cave. Photo by Ray Boren.

Stone tower in Nine Mile Canyon. Photo by Ray Boren.

mentioned in the 1937 account, and it can be assumed that it was not among the items collected from the same cave with the necklace, puppy, and baskets, that is, it was not Rasmussen Cave.

- Gaumer was probably never in Desolation Canyon: the canyon was not accessible by road at that time (and except for Sand Wash, it still isn't today), and the only access would have been by boat or horseback, both arduous means of transport that surely would have been noted. Gaumer mentions neither boats nor horses in his report. But Nine Mile Canyon was accessible by road at the time. As we can see from a closer reading of the 1937 report, he never actually states that he was in Desolation Canyon but instead refers to a "labyrinth of gulches leading off the canyon proper" (1937:160), although Nine Mile Canyon is a bit bigger than a "gulch."

- Gaumer mentions in the 1937 report that he conducted excavations at a "slab house ruin" where grayware and black-on-white potsherds were found (1937:160). The term "slab house" was used frequently at the time to describe open residential sites where the structure walls were erected in courses of sandstone. These sites are almost nonexistent in Desolation Canyon itself but are common along permanent streams like Nine Mile Creek. The Nine Mile rock art photos raise the distinct possibility that the slab house was actually in Nine Mile Canyon.

By 1937, Gaumer would have had ample opportunity to peruse Reagan's and Beckwith's 1931 accounts of the Rasmussen Cave excavations, both of which could have been read to suggest that the cave had been dug by rank amateurs interested only in artifacts and not science. Alfred Gaumer was clearly a scrupulous fellow who excavated with care and precision (by 1931 standards), and he described artifacts in great detail, including those of interest only to archaeologists, such as corncobs, beans, and fragments of pottery. And he decried looting, writing, "It is the duty of conscientious field workers to employ every endeavor to put a stop to all vandalism" (1937:161).

Were Gaumer's accounts belated attempts to set the record straight? We will probably never know. We do not know who Alfred Gaumer was, how he came to be in Nine Mile Canyon, or what his qualifications were to conduct the excavations. The location of the artifacts is unknown, although if Reagan's account is to be believed, the trove was divided up and the artifacts eventually lost. There is nothing in Gaumer's account to indicate that he had the artifacts from Rasmussen Cave in his possession. He did have the baby burial from Big Wash Cave, described in the 1939 report, but these items were later destroyed. "The fact that this cave find was later destroyed by the burning of my home has brought to me forcefully the lesson that the only place for valuable archaeological objects is in a museum where they can be protected and preserved," he wrote (1939:140).

Albert B. Reagan

There is no doubt that early researchers in Nine Mile Canyon were aware of its overwhelming abundance of rock art sites. They are mentioned by Henry Montgomery (1894), Morss (1931a), and Scott (1931a), but only in passing. Rock art is notoriously difficult to study in the context of scientific theory, and even today it is commonly ignored by serious academic researchers. But that certainly didn't stop others from embracing rock art as an important part of the prehistory of Nine Mile Canyon. And no one embraced it more than Albert B. Reagan, an Iowa native and teacher in the U.S. Indian Field Service in Ouray, Utah, who initiated archaeological investigations in northeastern Utah under the auspices of the Laboratory of Anthropology in Santa Fe, New Mexico. This research was begun in 1930,

ABOVE, Albert B. Reagan around 1934. Photo used with the permission of Special Collections, Harold B. Lee Library, Brigham Young University.

BELOW, Albert B. Reagan chalking rock art in Nine Mile Canyon in the early 1930s. Chalking of art images is no longer an acceptable practice. Photo courtesy of the Uintah County Regional History Center, Vernal, Utah.

continued through at least 1934, and was concentrated largely in the Uinta Basin, Nine Mile Canyon, and Hill Creek Canyon (Reagan 1931a–k; 1932a, b; 1933b–d, f; 1934b; 1935a). Reagan retired from the Indian Field Service on June 30, 1934, and subsequently joined Brigham Young University (Tanner 1939), although he was not a member of the Mormon faith.

According to Brigham Young University researcher Julianna Bratt, who has been investigating the Reagan legacy, Reagan was inherently curious. Although trained in geology—in 1925, he received a Ph.D. in geology from Stanford University at the age of 54—he wrote about a wide variety of topics, from weather to plants to history and geology. He also wrote extensively on Native American cultures, collecting oral histories and describing rituals and healing ceremonies. He studied and wrote about the Ute peoples, and he paid special attention to their rock art. A 1934 entry in the *Encyclopedia of American Biography* credits him with 547 publications (Allison 2010). In that sense, Reagan was a throwback to an earlier generation of scholars akin to Henry Montgomery or Byron Cummings—individuals trained in other disciplines who embraced archaeology as a passion. Bratt believes Reagan's interest in archaeology may have stemmed from his first Indian Field Service posting, at age 28, to New Mexico, a land rich in archaeological ruins. By 1930, at almost 60 years of age, he had landed in Ouray in the Uinta Basin as a teacher among the Utes (Julianna Bratt, personal communication 2011).

Although Reagan was not an institutionally trained archaeologist or anthropologist, his long career with the Indian Field Service apparently instilled in him an insatiable appetite for both archaeological and ethnographic investigations. He was a prolific writer, publishing his findings quickly in a wide variety of natural history journals across America and Canada—findings that were then available for other researchers to cite, thereby lending credibility to his research. There is little evidence as to what his more formally trained contemporaries—academics like Donald Scott and Julian Steward—thought of Reagan, although Steward afforded him some begrudging respect, coupled with backhanded criticisms. They were certainly acquainted, but they were hardly friends and even traded insults about each other's excavation techniques (Allison 2010).

In an April 1931 letter to Donald Scott, Steward described Reagan as "a rather strange man, egocentric in a way, but none the less intelligent."

LEFT, Artifacts from the Leo Thorne Collection. Thorne was Reagan's partner in the Nine Mile expeditions. Photo courtesy of the Uinta County Regional History Center, Vernal, Utah.

ABOVE, Leo Thorne was an accomplished photographer who accompanied Albert Reagan on his many archaeological expeditions. Photo courtesy of the Uintah County Regional History Center, Vernal, Utah.

Steward even proposed a collaboration involving Harvard, the University of Utah, and Reagan, suggesting that together they could "concentrate on an area somewhat larger than [Harvard] alone could undertake and that we could use the University's name and Reagan's knowledge of the Uintah basin" (in Allison 2010:6). This collaboration never occurred.

Reagan conducted numerous excavations in Nine Mile Canyon, although he never mentions why he believed himself to be qualified to do so, nor is there much indication of what became of the artifacts he recovered. In some instances Reagan indicated that he had shipped artifacts to the Laboratory of Anthropology in Santa Fe, although others probably ended up in the possession of his assistant, Leo Thorne. Julianna Bratt has found no evidence that Reagan was ever formally trained in archaeological excavation techniques. One possibility is that he was trained by Leo Thorne, a skilled Uinta Basin photographer and well-known collector who accompanied Reagan on his many field trips in northeastern Utah. It is clear that Reagan paid at least some attention to stratigraphic context and superimposition of deposits—something that would have been ignored by pothunters but second nature to a geologist.

Did his excavations adhere to the emerging professional standards of the day? Reagan undoubtedly thought so, although Steward probably thought not. Steward had criticized the quality of Reagan's work at sites along the Uinta River, although he did not name Reagan specifically (Steward 1933). In return, Reagan later took a swipe at the quality of Steward's work at sites near Provo, writing that the mounds had been "more or less excavated by the University of Utah party in 1932, under Dr. Julian H. Steward" (Reagan 1935a:66). Bratt believes that

> Reagan perceived himself as an archaeologist, as far as the term was conceived at the time. It was never his full-time interest though, unless you count his two years as a professor at BYU. He published frequently, and seems to have been well read and aware of what was going on in the field. I don't think he considered archaeology as an entirely separate distinction from the rest of the research he did. I don't believe that he ever thought of his work as amateur [personal communication, 2011].

While Reagan's speculative interpretations have sometimes been disparaged by later investigators (Gunnerson 1957:2, 1969:15), his reports nonetheless contain valuable early descriptions, photographs, and sketches. For example, Reagan appears to have been the only researcher to describe earthen lodges on the valley floor of Nine Mile Canyon and the presence of prehistoric irrigation ditches (1931f, 1931j:46, 1931k:240), which are no longer visible due to successive generations of extensive cultivation. His site descriptions included a combination of personal observations, comparisons with cultural manifestations in other areas, and interviews with the early residents of the region.

Reagan's propensity to speculate, a trait particularly prevalent in his later writings (e.g., 1934a, 1935b, 1935c, 1937), has since undermined the credibility of his descriptive reports. To his credit, Reagan argued forcefully for a Fremont culture separate from the better-known Ancestral Puebloans, calling the Fremont a "quasi-Pueblo culture" that "never took on the orthodox Pueblo characteristics, as we know them in the Southwest" (1933a:65–66). He also recognized a Fremont presence in Wyoming and Idaho (1933a:65).

Unlike most para-archaeologists of the day, Reagan kept meticulous notes (now archived at the Museum of Peoples and Cultures at Brigham Young University). Many of the photographs taken during the 1930–1932 field seasons are on file with the Laboratory of Anthropology, Museum of New Mexico, in Santa Fe (Powers 1990:1). Reagan's published papers are located at Brigham Young University. Additional manuscript copies of

The Owl Panel is among the most popular tourist attractions in Nine Mile Canyon. Photo by Ray Boren.

Reagan's reports are on file with the Laboratory of Anthropology in Santa Fe. An incomplete bibliography of Reagan's numerous publications can be found in an obituary—he died in 1936—written by BYU zoologist Vasco Tanner, a fellow 1925 graduate of Stanford (Tanner 1939).

Reagan in Nine Mile Canyon

Reagan's first visit to Nine Mile Canyon occurred in the summer of 1931, at the same time that Frank Beckwith, Alfred Gaumer, and the Peabody Museum expedition would have been conducting their own investigations there. Reagan, assisted by Vernal photographer Leo C. Thorne—himself a skilled "private collector" famed throughout the region for his personal collection of artifacts and mummies—was immediately struck by the qualitative differences between rock art found in Nine Mile Canyon and that observed in the Ashley–Dry Fork areas near Vernal (Reagan 1931j:54–69, 1933a:58–65), as well as the similarities between the architecture found in Hill Creek Canyon, east of the Green River, and Nine Mile Canyon, west of the river. In Nine Mile Canyon, structures were observed from the valley floor to more than 500 feet above, which were "Puebloan, without question" (Reagan 1931h:369–370). One of these sites sounds strikingly similar to a site described by Henry Montgomery almost 30 years before: "One group of towers [in Nine Mile Canyon] is on top of a high mesa in an extremely dizzy situation. It is composed of three small stone circular structures, two of which are provided with roofs of heavy cedar logs and

Pig Rock (or to some, "Porky Pig Rock"), a popular attraction on the Nine Mile Road. Photo by Ray Boren.

heavy flat stones. The logs and poles of these two structures would make about a cord of wood" (1931h:369).

Among Reagan's Nine Mile Canyon observations were rock art scenes of "turkeys being herded, turkeys in corrals [and] turkeys being fed corn" (1931h:370). He noted the scantiness of the predominantly plain-gray pottery (1931h:370), the existence of prehistoric irrigation ditches (1931j:66), and the presence of earthen lodges on the valley floor. Although he observed no undisturbed earthen lodges, from the clay remains of the lodges it would seem that they were wick-iup [lattice, wattle-work] houses that were plastered over with mud, probably not much unlike the earth lodges of certain western tribes, or for example, the familiar winter hogan of the Navajos, except that they were differently constructed. It was further noticeable, on examining the clay plaster, that the lodges had been destroyed by fire, leaving imprints of limbs, thatch, brush, and poles on the brick-like clay [1931j:46].

Reagan returned to Nine Mile Canyon in 1932, investigating various cave sites (1933d) and rock art sites (1933a:58–65). Assisting Reagan during the 1932 field season were Thorne, G. G. Frazier of the U.S. Geological Survey in Salt Lake City, and Dr. J. Marion Francke of Vernal (Reagan 1933a:66). The 1932 research in Nine Mile Canyon focused on the segment of the canyon from 3 miles below Nutter's ranch house to Cottonwood Canyon, about 12 miles below the ranch (1933a:55). An additional cliff structure was described, as were five cave sites, including Rasmussen Cave. This report provided the best description of artifacts removed from the cave, probably by Gaumer, just before the arrival of the Claflin-Emerson Expedition (1933a:57–58). Reagan apparently did not conduct excavations at Rasmussen Cave but carried out some level of excavation at the other four caves he described.

At least 21 additional rock art sites were superficially described in 1932. Among the panels were the "Praying Goat" panels around Rasmussen Cave, which were compared with similar motifs in Hill Creek Canyon (Reagan 1933a:60); a hump-backed flute player near Rasmussen Cave (1933a:62); the Sandhill Crane Panel at Currant Canyon (1933a:63); and the Great Hunt Panel in Cottonwood Canyon, called by Reagan the "Animal Group" (1933a:61; see bottom figure on p. 70). There are repeated references to snakes and the horned-snake motif (1933a:63, 1933e:551, 1937:44), which "seem to represent the use of an effigy snake... somewhat resembling the complete plumed diamondbacked snake drawing, the plumed snake drawings of the Southwest and the drawings and carvings of the Great Plumed Serpent of Mexico and Yucatan" (1933a:64).

Reagan returned to Nine Mile Canyon in October 1934 in the company of prominent Utah historian Charles Kelly, offering additional

"Praying Goats" rock art panel at Rasmussen Cave, first described by Reagan in 1932. Photo by Ray Boren.

"Animal Group" panel, better known as the Great Hunt, in Cottonwood Canyon. Reagan conducted excavations at the shelter next to this site. Photo by Ray Boren.

commentary on sites previously described, as well as on 18 rock art sites not mentioned earlier (Reagan 1935a:53–57). A two-story cliff structure described by Reagan as the "most northern cliff house in North America" was located near the "Augler place"; Reagan offered a footnote that Augler had offered to deed the site to the federal government or the state in order to protect it from vandals (1935a:53). He also described a "fort" near the Preston Nutter Ranch with a defensive wall 69 feet long that enclosed two large open structures, one circular and the other oval (1935a:53–54).

Following the 1932 visit to Nine Mile Canyon, Reagan began synthesizing and interpreting his findings. Regarding the earthen lodges in Nine Mile Canyon, as well as those in the Uinta Basin, he wrote that prehistoric peoples

> built wattle-and-daub jacal walled houses.... Each lodge had at least four support posts, a post being set at each corner of the squarish or rectangular enclosure. The posts probably were crotched at their upper ends and carried stringers which, in turn, supported the smaller beams and also the sloping walls, which were plastered over wattle work,

Cottonwood Village, at the mouth of Cottonwood Canyon. Photo by Ray Boren.

the mud often having been daubed over it to a thickness of four or more inches. The roofs were flat and made of the same mud-daubed lattice work. The floor was of hard-packed earth, was blackened and smoothed with a raised, burned, mud-clay fireplace in its center [1933f:3–4].

Reagan hypothesized that the first occupants were Basketmakers characterized by long-headed crania, use of the atlatl, and a preference for caves and rockshelters near the valley floor. The Basketmakers were confined largely to Ashley–Dry Fork Canyon and to Nine Mile Canyon (1933f:3). Toward the end of the Basketmaker period, "a Pueblo people,... to the west and southwest of the Wasatch Mountains, gradually pushed eastward into the Uintah Basin," where they built wattle-and-daub houses (1933f:3).

In addition to wattle-and-daub houses on the valley floor in Nine Mile Canyon, these people constructed solid-walled structures, irrigation ditches, and storage reservoirs. Reagan, who enthusiastically subscribed to Neil Judd's (1926) hypotheses of culture development in Utah, believed this occurred during Pueblo II times, during which the people also

raised corn and pumpkins.... Scattered about their houses are milling, hammer, hand-hammer and smoothing stones, arrow points, quantities of chipped material, stone plug-stoppers for jars, stone knives, lance or spear heads, stone drills, an occasional pestle, gaming balls, an occasional whole jar [found in excavations], stone agricultural instruments

This site was labeled NP-10 by Reagan in 1931 and was illustrated in one of his reports. Reagan interpreted the scene as a group of 11 men playing a game of "shinny." Photo by Ray Boren.

and fragments of coarse, undecorated, smoothed, gray pottery [Reagan 1933f:4].

Reagan cited the rock art with Puebloan elements superimposed over the Basketmaker panels as additional evidence of a Puebloan migration into the area. He noted scenes in Hill Creek Canyon of "men carrying the image of the horned snake, kachina scenes and women with whorled hair as Hopi virgins wear their hair at the present time" (1933f:6), and he described scenes in Nine Mile Canyon purportedly depicting ceremonies with masked participants (1935b), horned or plumed serpents (1937), and domesticated turkeys (1931j:55–57).

In both the Hill Creek and Nine Mile Canyon regions, Reagan believed a concentration of population occurred, "apparently for protection" (1933f:4). Dwellings were associated with towers and "forts," often on prominent points that offered commanding views of the valleys, side canyons, and mesa tops. One structure was only four feet in diameter but seven feet in height. At least two such structures had roofs of heavy cedar beams covered by large flat stones. Many are so situated as to be virtually inaccessible, and most such sites would have been easily defensible. Reagan also made reference to "proto-Kayenta polychrome potsherds and others having proto-Kayenta barbed lines" (1933f:5).

Reagan speculated that the Puebloans of Nine Mile and Hill Creek Canyons were attempting to protect themselves from groups "affiliated with the Shoshonean family, if they were not Shoshoneans themselves." These Shoshoneans are recognized in the archaeological record only

through their "round-bodied drawings of humans…after the round faces of the sun and moon" (1933f:6).

The fourth and last group to arrive in the region were the Fremont peoples (Reagan called them Head Hunters),

> who appear to be an amalgamation of peoples, including Basketmakers and apparently some peoples of the Shoshonean family, more or less allied with the ancient peoples from which the present Ute-Chemehuevi people have descended. They were, however, out of the mainstream of Southwestern pueblo culture and probably never stood nearer that culture in their day than the Navajo culture of our day stands to the Hopi-Pueblo cultures [1933f:7].

This group, he believed, was responsible for the distinctive Fremont-style petroglyphs, dewclaw moccasins, figurines, and woven water jugs. They were considered by Reagan to be contemporaneous with Morss's Fremont culture of the Fremont River (1933f:6–7).

This site near the mouth of Gate Canyon was labeled NP-3-A by Reagan in 1931. It has since been redocumented by Colorado Plateau Archaeological Alliance. Photo by Ray Boren.

These petroglyphs in Cottonwood Canyon were described by Reagan in 1933. Photo by Ray Boren.

Given what archaeologists have learned since Reagan offered his ideas—all without the benefit of radiocarbon or tree-ring dating—how do his speculations hold up? In some respects, surprisingly well. Brigham Young University researchers, working in the Steinaker Gap area east of Vernal, have made a convincing argument that the first farmers in northeastern Utah, at about AD 200, were very Basketmaker-like and could well have been Basketmaker immigrants from the San Juan River region (Talbot and Richens 1996). Other researchers point to a collapse of cultural barriers around AD 900 in which cultural manifestations north of the Colorado River became indistinguishable from those to the south (Geib 1996; Madsen and Simms 1998; Talbot 2000)—a phenomenon not inconsistent with Reagan's proposed Pueblo II migration into Nine Mile Canyon at the same time. And some archaeologists have long argued that one explanation for the defensive sites during this period could have been the arrival of Ancestral Utes (see Madsen and Rhode 1994), as Reagan proposed.

Where Reagan got it wrong was the Fremont occupation. He placed it after the Pueblo II expansion, when in fact it had been present throughout northeastern Utah centuries before and may have continued uninterrupted throughout the Pueblo II period, when Nine Mile Canyon could have been occupied by many different groups with different identities. And his assumptions that the Fremont peoples were related to the Ancestral Utes has not stood the test of DNA evidence, which shows more of a genetic relationship between the Fremont and Ancestral Puebloans (Carlyle et al. 2000).

Efforts are currently under way to relocate and redocument the sites Reagan described in his numerous reports. Through liberal application of deductive reasoning and careful reading of published notes and photographs, I have identified nearly 50 of Reagan's sites, including 10 in the Gate Canyon area. Of the nine rock art sites described by Reagan's 1933 report (1933a) in Cottonwood Canyon along the west side of the road, I have identified seven with a high degree of confidence (Spangler 2008, 2009), including Reagan's N-P36, which he described as "34 goats being attacked by four hunters with bows and arrows" (1933a:61). This is clearly a reference to the Great Hunt Panel (42Cb239), perhaps the most iconic rock art site in Nine Mile Canyon and a destination for hundreds of tourists every year.

"Not a Single Specimen"

The plethora of archaeological excavations and expeditions to Utah in the late 1920s and early 1930s predictably came to the attention of state officials, who bemoaned that Utah specimens were being "distributed world-wide, and at present there remains not a single specimen for the State of Utah" (Strevell and Pulver 1935:i). Of course, this was a gross exaggeration, since Byron Cummings and Andrew Kerr had spent the better part of 20 years stocking the new museum at the University of Utah with spectacular artifacts, mostly from San Juan County. But it highlighted growing concerns among the state's politicos and policymakers that Utah's antiquities were being spirited away to distant museums when they should remain in Utah. Two important things resulted from this concern.

Through the efforts of the Utah State Museum Association, the Utah Legislature banned "all exploration and excavations for, as well as prohibiting the removal of, prehistoric relics from the state without a permit from the State Parks Commissioners" (Strevell and Pulver 1935:c),

Human figures with shoulders broader than the waist, called trapezoidal anthropomorphs, are characteristic of the Fremont rock art tradition throughout Utah. Photo by Ray Boren.

marking Utah's first requirements that archaeologists have permits to do their research. And in 1934, the State Planning Board, with funding from the Utah Emergency Relief Administration, commissioned the Utah State Museum Association Expedition to conduct a statewide reconnaissance to determine the extent of the state's archaeological and paleontological resources. The expedition began its efforts on September 1, 1934, in the Uinta Basin area and concluded on February 15, 1935, in the Capitol Reef area. It was supervised by C. S. Pulver, secretary of the Utah State Museum Association, and included among its participants archaeologist Grant G. Cannon and photographer Dr. J. E. Broaddus. The expedition reached Nine Mile Canyon (date unknown) under the guidance of newspaperman Frank Beckwith, who already knew the canyon well.

In the Nine Mile Canyon cliffs, the expedition's unpublished report briefly mentions round storage structures made of white adobe and roofed with poles and woven willow matting (Strevell and Pulver 1935:15). The expedition investigated Rasmussen Cave (42Cb16), although the report describes little more than rock art in and around the cave. Elsewhere in the canyon, the expedition commented on pictographs of white, red, green, black, and gray-blue and noted a petroglyph "which shows a human herding a group of what appear to be turkeys." The panel was associated with petroglyphs of bird tracks (1935:15A). The report also mentions the presence of "forts" in the canyon, "the highest of which, at the present time, rises to a height of about six feet" (1935:15). None of the towers or forts had superstructures, and all were on high ledges.

A fall scene in Nine Mile Canyon. Photo by Ray Boren.

The report of the expedition was apparently filed away and forgotten until I stumbled across a typewritten manuscript of it in about 2002 in the archives at the Utah State Historical Society. It was missing the photographs, rendering it largely useless for research purposes. In 2010, the museum expedition photo collection was inadvertently discovered by archivists at the Marriott Library at the University of Utah—along with a finely bound, typewritten manuscript. Efforts are being made to edit and publish the notes and photographs so the "forgotten expedition" can assume its rightful place in the pantheon of early Utah archaeological investigations.

Whether intentional or not, the 1933 law protecting Utah's archaeological treasures, and the 1935 regulations requiring archaeologists to demonstrate their educational qualifications and a reason to conduct excavations, brought to an end the era of para-professionals digging into Utah's prehistory with impunity. And while amateurs would continue to play a significant role in archaeological research in Nine Mile Canyon for decades to come, their participation was, in most instances, limited to surface survey and site documentation.

5

A Higher Scientific Standard
The Arrival of John Gillin

We weren't able to work on the Virgin River sites, hence retired sulkily to Nine Mile Canyon where we excavated house sites. —JOHN GILLIN TO DONALD SCOTT, AUGUST 12, 1936

Sky House to Valley Village: The Gillin Investigations

The early 1930s may have been the halcyon days of archaeological interest in Nine Mile Canyon, but the attention was short-lived, and through happenstance the archaeology of the canyon remained largely unknown to the outside world. Certainly, Noel Morss had mentioned the canyon briefly in his classic monograph on the Fremont culture (1931a), but it played a minor part, both in the publication and in the development of his concept of Fremont culture. Albert Reagan had also published a few short articles, mainly in various regional natural history journals (1931h, 1931j, 1933a, 1933e, 1935a), but these did not have wide circulation, nor did they have the panache of academic research. Donald Scott never got around to writing up a manuscript on his 1931 investigations in Nine Mile Canyon, and his field notes, as well as those of other Claflin-Emerson Expedition participants, remained largely forgotten in the archives of the Peabody Museum for the next 35 years. Likewise, Julian Steward never published a report of his 1931 foray into the canyon, although he briefly mentioned the archaeology there (1940).

The failure of university researchers to share their insights into the ubiquitous, albeit perplexing, archaeology of Nine Mile Canyon resulted in an intellectual void—everyone, it seemed, knew about Nine Mile Canyon, but none in the academic world had bothered to put their musings to pen and paper. This was rectified by the publication in 1938 of John Gillin's *Archaeological Investigations in Nine Mile Canyon, Utah (During the Year 1936)*. Not only was it the first major treatise to address Nine Mile Canyon, but Gillin's research marked a watershed moment in Utah archaeology because of the tree-ring samples he collected. The dates they produced would profoundly influence a future generation of scholars who believed, reasonably but erroneously, that the time span of the Fremont culture

OPPOSITE, Warrior Ridge. Photo by Ray Boren.

throughout Utah could be defined from about AD 950 to 1200—a narrow range predicated in large part on the Nine Mile Canyon tree-ring dates.

John Phillip Gillin

John Phillip Gillin. Photo courtesy of the University of Pittsburgh.

As laudatory as Gillin's research in Nine Mile Canyon was and remains today, it almost never occurred. Gillin had no real interest in joining the University of Utah after earning a doctorate at Harvard University, but he reconsidered because of health concerns that kept him from staying in the East. And when the opportunity arose to initiate fieldwork, Nine Mile Canyon was anything but a priority. Gillin had instead set his sights on relatively unknown Ancestral Puebloan sites in the St. George area, a project that was to have been funded through the Works Progress Administration (WPA), the largest and most ambitious of the New Deal programs to arise during the Great Depression. As Gillin wrote in an August 12, 1936, letter to Donald Scott, the WPA funding fell through and "we weren't able to work on the Virgin River sites, hence retired sulkily to Nine Mile Canyon where we excavated house sites" (Gillin 1936e).

John "Jack" Gillin, like his predecessor Julian Steward, arrived at the University of Utah with no real experience in the archaeology of the Colorado Plateau or Great Basin. And although both embraced archaeology during their short tenures at the university, neither were dyed-in-the-wool archaeologists. Steward's passion was the study of Paiute and Ute peoples; Gillin's was the study of human interactions, in particular the acculturation of native peoples of South America. Anthropology was a passion that later led to national prominence and his election as president of both the Society for Applied Anthropology and the American Anthropological Association (Reina 1976).

John P. Gillin was born in Waterloo, Iowa, in 1907, a year after his father, John L. Gillin, an ordained minister with the Church of the Brethren, earned a Ph.D. in sociology from Columbia University. In 1912, the elder Gillin was offered a teaching position at the University of Wisconsin, where he remained for the next 46 years, earning international respect from several landmark publications, including *Social Pathology* and *Cultural Sociology*, which he wrote with his son John Phillip (1948).

Warrior Ridge petroglyphs.
Photo by Ray Boren.

Having been raised in Madison's vibrant university environment, Gillin not surprisingly had scholarly ambitions of his own. By age 20, he had earned a bachelor's degree in sociology from the University of Wisconsin, and three years later he had earned his master's degree in sociology, psychology, and anthropology from the same institution. During that interval, he accompanied his father on an around-the-world study of foreign penal systems, and he attended classes at the University of Berlin and the London School of Economics. In 1930, he participated in an archaeological expedition to Algeria, and later that year he signed on with an expedition led by the American School of Prehistoric Research to France, Spain, Switzerland, Germany, and Czechoslovakia, according to Gillin's vitae, which he later used to apply for the job at the University of Utah (1934b).

By 1931, Gillin had earned another master's degree (in anthropology), this one at Harvard University, and the following year he led an ethnographic expedition to the Mescalero Apaches in the American Southwest, and later, while collecting data for his Ph.D., he led a Harvard University ethnographic expedition to the Barama River Caribs of British Guiana. Somehow, despite his many travels and university responsibilities, he found time to hold teaching positions at New York University and Sarah Lawrence College. In 1934, he was awarded his doctorate, and soon thereafter he set out to conduct ethnographic studies in Ecuador. It was in Ecuador that Gillin became gravely ill with what was described at the time as a case of malaria coupled with possible tuberculosis (Gillin 1934b, 1935b).

The seriousness of the illness is not clearly evident in the available correspondence, although it was dire enough that Gillin—who at that time had

Large elk figure at Warrior Ridge. Photo by Ray Boren.

already accepted a teaching position at the University of Cincinnati effective upon his return from Ecuador—admitted he was "thoroughly scared into believing that the change was absolutely necessary for the health standpoint." The change he referred to was articulated in a June 24, 1935, letter to University of Utah president George Thomas:

> Since returning from South America I have been under doctor's care for malaria contracted there. The medical men think there may be some lung trouble. I am going into the hospital tomorrow for a week to take some tests which will definitely determine whether there is any tuberculosis or not. If there is, I shall have to withdraw from teaching for a year. If there isn't, the doctor advises change of climate to the Southwest and a lighter schedule of work than at Cincinnati [Gillin 1935b].

President Thomas had met John Gillin earlier during a trip to Harvard, and Gillin had made an impression, even though he had expressed no interest at that time in the Utah vacancy created by the departure of Julian Steward. After returning from Ecuador, Gillin had a change of heart, querying in a June 7 telegram to the Department of Anthropology and Sociology as to whether the position was still open (Gillin 1935a) (there is no record of a response from the department), and on June 24 he followed up with a personal letter to President Thomas expressing his desire to be considered for the position (Gillin 1935b). Thomas immediately responded to Gillin's handwritten letter, touting Utah as the best place for Gillin's convalescence (1935a). Thomas also wrote to Gillin's father enlisting his support in the recruitment of his son (1935b; see also J. L. Gillin 1935) and to the University of Cincinnati seeking Gillin's "honorable release" from his teaching commitment there (1935c). On June 27, Thomas wrote to Gillin:

> First, I think you would be a very satisfactory man to us. Second, if you have a touch of malaria this would be a good section of the country for you to come to because we are free of that disease here. Third, if your lungs, through your experience in South America, have a tendency to be tubercular, this is a high and dry climate and you could

spend a good share of your time in the open during the next few years, especially during the summer when you could go out in archaeological and ethnographical research work in the state, where the atmosphere is clear and dry. It is true that we have some smoke in Salt Lake City during the winter, but you could arrange to get a residence where that would not trouble [1935a].

Thomas offered Gillin an annual salary of $2,100, with a bonus of $300 to $400 a year more if he conducted summer field research. After consulting with and receiving strong encouragement from Donald Scott, at that time director of the Peabody Museum, Gillin accepted the position on July 2, 1935, conditional upon his release from the University of Cincinnati (1935c). That release came three days later (see Gillin 1935d), and on July 9 Thomas sent Gillin a telegram confirming the appointment (1935d).

Utah may not have been Gillin's first choice, but he embraced the opportunity. As he wrote to President Thomas: "I am very enthusiastic about your plans in Anthropology and Sociology at the University of Utah. Owing to the large amount of work which the Peabody Museum has done in the area and to the personal interest of Mr. Scott in the archaeology of the region I am sure that I shall have a pretty good general idea of the technical problems and local conditions before coming" (Gillin 1935c).

Gillin may have arrived at the University of Utah with a "general idea" of the lay of the land, but during the next two years he turned often to Donald Scott and the Peabody Museum for insight into Utah's archaeology. When it came time to prepare the Nine Mile monograph for publication, Scott and John Otis Brew provided regular critiques. And both men, along with Noel Morss, later played a key role in the publication by the Peabody Museum of a second Gillin monograph on Utah archaeology, *Archaeological Investigations in Central Utah: Joint Expedition of the University of Utah and the Peabody Museum, Harvard University* (Gillin 1941).

Gillin assumed his university duties in the late summer of 1935, and the conditions he found must have been disappointing to a young scholar accustomed to the trappings of the Peabody Museum. In a September 18 letter to Julian Steward, Gillin wrote that field equipment was missing and that "the museum is in a state verging on chaos due to the fact that it has

University of Utah President George Thomas. Photo courtesy of Special Collections, Marriott Library, University of Utah.

Warrior scene at Warrior Ridge.
Photo by Ray Boren.

been used as a store-room for furniture during alterations made on the Park Building" (Gillin 1935e).

Protecting Utah Treasures

The fieldwork would have to wait. President Thomas instead assigned him a political task. The 1933 Utah Legislature passed the state's first law protecting archaeological resources (Revised Statute 1933, Chapter 14), placing the authority to enforce the new law within the domain of the Utah Parks Board. The Parks Board then turned to the university to make recommendations on how the law should be implemented. The university asked Gillin, who wrote letters to Byron Cummings and Julian Steward seeking their advice (1935e, 1935f). He also researched archaeological protection statutes, or lack thereof, in fourteen other states. In an October 4, 1935, letter to Thomas, Gillin (1935g) outlined his recommendations:

- The enforcement of Utah's new antiquities law should be the domain of local law enforcement officials.

- A series of press releases should be sent to newspapers throughout the state explaining the reason for the law and soliciting public cooperation.

- Utah high school teachers should be given materials to instruct their pupils on the proper care of prehistoric deposits.

- The issuance of archaeological survey and excavation permits should be vested in a state archaeological board or the University of Utah since it "possesses the best facilities for the study of archaeology in the state."

- Fifty percent of all archaeological materials recovered by institutions outside the state should be deposited at a Utah institution, although this requirement could be waived in special circumstances.

- A full report should be required of every archaeological excavation conducted in the state within six months. "This report should comprise a full copy of the field notes and a full catalog of every artifact removed from any site whatsoever. Only in this way can the state be in a position to check technique used by excavators and to know the full distribution of the various types of culture discovered."

- The University Museum, with legislative approval, should be designated the official State Museum for the deposition of Utah's 50 percent share of cultural materials removed by outside institutions.

Two warriors at Warrior Ridge. There are more than 100 images of individuals in apparent combat along this ridge. Photo by Ray Boren.

Gillin appears to have had second thoughts. Four days later, he sent Thomas a second letter hedging somewhat on his recommendation that local lawmen be granted authority to enforce the antiquities law. He had just received correspondence from Alfred V. Kidder at the Peabody Museum strongly advising against a law enforcement component; as Gillin (1935h) put it, "in his opinion…such laws are un-enforceable and frequently cause bad feelings."

Gillin advised President Thomas:

I have a feeling that more can probably be done through personal contacts between the University archaeologist, state archaeologist, or some other qualified official, and influential individuals throughout the state who are interested in archaeology. In addition, a campaign of public education through publicity in the newspapers and in the high schools would tend to create good will toward the project. Of course, either of these methods would cost something, but it seems reasonable to believe that they would cost less than a series of unpopular prosecutions under the law [1935h].

In no small way, Gillin had predicted the public backlash that would occur in 1986 and again in 2009 when federal agents, working with local and state authorities, conducted sweeping raids throughout the Four Corners region, arresting dozens of people, including prominent members of rural communities, for looting ancient sites and selling their plunder for profit. The arrests sent an unequivocal message that looting of antiquities is against the law and will be vigorously prosecuted. But the resulting ill will also undermined long-standing efforts by "influential" members of local communities to avert looting through public education (O'Neill 2009).

It is unknown what influence Gillin's reservations about "law enforcement" had on the Utah Parks Board, but the final regulations state only that "a copy of the law and these regulations shall be furnished to all local police officers throughout the state" (Revised Statute 1933, Chapter 14). The implication is that state officials would leave it up to local police to enforce the law, but there was no mandate that they do so.

The regulations passed by the Parks Board embraced most of Gillin's other recommendations. The University Museum was established as the clearinghouse for all archaeological research and materials, and museum officials were placed in charge of approving archaeological research permits. Whether it was intentional or inadvertent, the final regulations also took a slap at the countless researchers who had failed to write up their findings. State regulations now required researchers to apply for a permit before they engaged in any investigation and to specify the exact location of their research, the purpose of their investigation, and their educational qualifications for conducting the research. And the Park Board imposed a strict deadline: every expedition must submit a detailed report to the University Museum no later than six months after completion of the fieldwork (Utah Parks Board 1935).

There is no record of whether the state ever embraced Gillin's recommendations for proactive public outreach in the local communities or in Utah high schools.

For the first time, Utah had a legal framework mandating that archaeological research be conducted to the highest scientific standards. It is

The "Sideshow Bob" panel at Warrior Ridge. Photo by Ray Boren.

not difficult to argue that John Gillin, more than any Utah archaeologist before that time, was responsible for establishing rigorous standards for professional archaeology in the state. These standards were, in concept, expressions of the state's frustration at out-of-state researchers—some of them legitimate and others not so much—hauling Utah antiquities to distant museums. The regulations were also targeted at the plethora of pseudo-archaeologists who were initiating excavations but had no formal training to do so.

In reality, it was difficult to enforce the new standards, and harder still for archaeologists, even those with the best intentions, to comply with the mandates. By the time Gillin left the University of Utah in 1937, he had conducted excavations around the state. If reports were ever written about those projects, most are now lost. In some instances the reports exist but not the photos and/or field notes.

A Happy Accident

Gillin arrived in Salt Lake City with no prior experience in Utah's prehistory, something that weighed on his conscience. And there were no local

For the ancient residents of Nine Mile Canyon, fall would have been a time for hunting deer, elk, and bighorn sheep. Photo by Ray Boren.

mentors to advise and encourage him. In a letter to Julian Steward shortly after his arrival, in which he sought Steward's suggestions on avenues for future research, he confessed, "This is my first experience in the Great Basin" (Gillin 1935e). On August 12, 1936, after returning from Nine Mile Canyon, he wrote to Donald Scott:

> When all is said and done I feel that there is still too much that I don't know about Southwestern Archaeology—a good deal that can't be obtained from published sources. Since my previous experience as an archaeologist had been in North Africa and Europe and my interests had been in ethnology, there are a good many angles on the Southwest which have to be learned. And since this place is so isolated that I never get to see another anthropologist, I have to teach myself, which is somewhat inefficient. I make this sad lament so that you won't mistake for delusions of grandeur whatever unconscious ineptitudes are displayed in the paper when I send it to you [Gillin 1936e].

Misgivings aside, Gillin initiated excavations in Utah shortly after his arrival. He began at prehistoric mounds about three miles north of Nephi, using the excavations to train archaeology students in field techniques. In the same letter to Scott, Gillin indicated that he had been excavating one of 19 prehistoric mounds in an 80-acre field.

> Specimens came from mound No. 4 of our dig which we excavated quite thoroughly, although not completely, owing to the shortage of time. House set on small platform, no excavation of house, four posts, walls and roof (former and latter presumably forming truncated top) made in the style of Grantsville and Willard with adobe plastered over interwoven brush and grass supported on four-posted wooden frame. Fireplace with partial clay rim in the center. Other details and photographs can be supplied when report is finished [1936e].

After a brief leave of absence in December 1935 to attend annual meetings of the American Sociological Society in New York City (Gillin 1935i; Thomas 1935e), Gillin spent the most of the winter and early spring researching options for fieldwork the following summer. At some point, Gillin made a scouting trip to San Juan County, visited Poncho House, and met Norman Nevills, an "amateur archaeologist" and famed Colorado River boatman. Nevills proposed to outfit and guide an archaeological expedition along the Colorado River into the Red Canyon and Dark Canyon areas—in exchange for half the artifacts recovered (Gillin 1936e; see also Scott 1936b). This partnership never materialized.

In particular, Gillin sought out the advice of Donald Scott, who in April 1936 strongly encouraged Gillin to investigate the archaeologically unknown St. George area, something that would "fill a hole in our knowledge" (Scott 1936a; see also Gillin 1936b–d). Scott also suggested a more thorough examination of massive Fremont village sites at Paragonah and Parowan that had earlier been investigated by Neil Judd (1926), and a reinvestigation of a cave site at Promontory Point. Scott later encouraged Gillin to reexamine the "adobe-walled houses of the Duchesne River" that had been described by Steward (1933) and Reagan (1931k). Scott believed this area would provide "valuable clues as to the extension of both Basketmaker and Pueblo, and also possibly on the entrance of the Pueblo into the Southwest" (1936b).

Gillin soon set out to see the St. George region firsthand. From April 23 to 25, he was given a tour by three local "amateur archaeologists" who

Warrior scenes commonly depict humans with shields, clubs, and spears. Photo by Ray Boren.

had earlier accompanied university archaeologist Elmer Smith in a broad-ranging reconnaissance of the region. Gillin explored the Santa Clara River as well as sites in the Bloomington and Washington City areas. Most of the sites had been badly looted, and he believed them to have minimal potential for intact, stratified deposits. But four sites near the Shivwits Indian Reservation caught his attention. Not only were they undisturbed; they were close to the road but far enough removed from "meddlers." And they were located on federal land, which afforded "freedom from possible difficulties concerning division of collections that might arise with private owners" (Gillin 1936b).

There is a dearth of correspondence to or from Gillin in the months after April 1936, which is not unusual since he had expressed his desire to commence fieldwork along the Santa Clara River in June of that year. What is more puzzling is why those plans were aborted. And why did he instead divert his attention to Nine Mile Canyon, which had not even been mentioned in the earlier correspondence? The only clues are in the August 12 letter to Donald Scott, in which he laments that the "W.P.A. Project for St. George fell through" and he wasn't able to work on the Santa Clara sites. His phrase "hence retired sulkily to Nine Mile Canyon" (1936e) implies that it was not his preferred choice.

How it came to be any choice at all remains unknown, although it was probably a financial decision. The expedition was supported by a small appropriation from the university's research fund, but it was apparently minimal. The four students who participated in the 1936 Nine Mile investigations—William Mulloy, Arden King, Carling Malouf, and John Stewart—all paid their own expenses. Gillin wrote, "Since the funds available were insufficient for hiring adequate manual labor, the assistance rendered by these young men had much to do with the amount of work accomplished" (1938:1).

Indeed, the expedition conducted an astonishing amount of work over a few weeks during the summer of 1936. Three major sites—Valley Village, Sky House, and Beacon Ridge—were excavated, all under the watchful eye of Gillin, whose exacting standards resulted in thorough descriptions of even obscure artifacts. And test excavations were conducted at more than a dozen other sites and features. Other sites were visited, but not all of the sites described in Gillin's monograph are known to archaeologists today.

This site (42Cb2013) in Cottonwood Canyon is mentioned only in passing by Gillin, who referred to it as a "cliff house." It is probably a large cliff granary. Photo courtesy of the Colorado Plateau Archaeological Alliance, Ogden, Utah.

Some, like the series of features known as Warrior Ridge, are now undergoing thorough documentation (Spangler 2011a).

Under Gillin, the University of Utah's 1936 excavations mark the most detailed examination of the archaeology of northeastern Utah to that time. Excavations were conducted at three sites, all within a 10-mile radius of the Ellis Ranch (Gillin 1938:5–6) and chosen to minimize the probability that cultural differences were due to environmental differences. The survey ranged from Sheep Canyon on the west to Cottonwood Canyon on the east, and at least 28 sites were briefly described (Gillin 1938:7).

The most significant contributions of the investigations are the detailed descriptions of Valley Village (42Cb4) and Sky House (42Cb1), both of them residential sites but radically different from each other in manner of construction and topographic setting. Valley Village was located on a small knoll next to the valley floor; Sky House was located on a ridge top almost 400 feet above the valley floor. The artifact assemblages at the two sites were virtually indistinguishable, suggesting they were probably occupied at the same time. The dichotomy of residential site location—some sites next to the valley floor and others far above it—has bedeviled researchers ever since.

Located on the south side of Nine Mile Creek near the mouth of Sheep Canyon, Valley Village (42Cb4) consisted of five "slab houses" arranged in roughly linear order (Gillin 1938:7–8; see top figure on p. 98). Two of the five were excavated, House B and House C. House B was a semi-subterranean structure, largely circular with stone slab walls averaging 2 feet 4 inches high. The north-south diameter was 21 feet 10 inches, and the

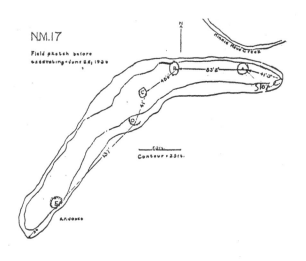

RIGHT, Gillin's site sketch of Valley Village, where five residential structures are situated along a narrow ridge just above the floodplain (Gillin 1938:4, Figure 2). Image courtesy of the University of Utah, Department of Anthropology.

BELOW, Gillin's sketch of the roof beams found at House B at Valley Village (Gillin 1938:7, Figure 4). Image courtesy of the University of Utah, Department of Anthropology.

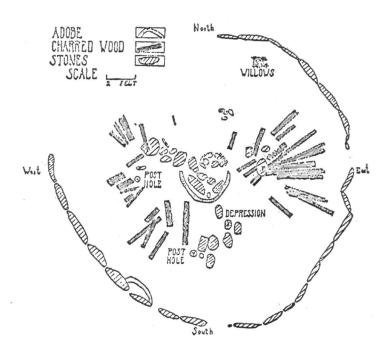

east-west diameter was 20 feet 3 inches. At least 37 charred beams were noted in the structure, all radiating in a general way from the center.

Gillin wrote:

It is assumed that the entire superstructure was covered with a thatch of interlaced willow stems laid over a matting of straw. Several pieces

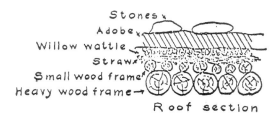

Stones
Adobe
Willow wattle
Straw
Small wood frame
Heavy wood frame →

Roof section

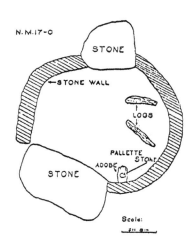

N.M.17-C

STONE

←STONE WALL

LOGS

PALLETTE
STONE

ADOBE

STONE

Scale:

of adobe, bearing the imprint of beams and willow, were found in the debris among the beams, indicating that the willow and grass thatch had been covered with a coating of adobe, which perhaps formed the exterior surface of the roof. No less than 30 stones were found scattered about the central part of the floor and fireplace, most of them lying above the charred beams [1938:10; see top figure].

Inside the structure, Gillin reported a central fire hearth with a semi-circular rim of red adobe 2 inches high, enclosing the south half of the fireplace. No whole pieces of pottery were found, and only one projectile point, possibly a spear point, was recovered. One perforated disk of shale was also found (1938:13).

House C, also semi-subterranean, was roughly 10 feet in diameter, but it differed from the slab construction of House B in that "water-worn boulders" were stacked on one another and sealed with clay. Only two charred beams were observed and no postholes. Further, "there was a notable absence of burned adobe in the debris, which might indicate that the adobe roof covering, inferred for House B, was not used here" (Gillin 1938:14).

Plain gray potsherds dominated the collection from both structures, as they did at neighboring Beacon Ridge. In a complaint repeated by many other researchers in Nine Mile Canyon, Gillin also noted: "We were handicapped first, by the lack of whole pots; second, by the relatively few sherds recovered, in spite of thorough sifting methods during excavations" (1938:20).

Additional excavations were conducted on a ridge about 400 yards east of Valley Village and about 110 feet above the valley floor. Called Beacon Ridge (42Cb3), the site consisted of a fireplace, a circular house structure, and slab-lined cists. A detached circular fireplace with an outside diameter of 2 feet 6 inches had been paved with flat stones and rimmed with water-worn cobblestones. To the south was found a circular stone "house" about 7 feet in diameter and featuring a clay floor. The walls were of slab-stone construction, although most stones had collapsed. In the center was a fireplace that had been paved with a single slab and rimmed with cobblestones (Gillin 1938:18).

Gillin was particularly struck by the defensive orientation of Sky House (42Cb1), located 365 feet above the valley floor. The ridge accessing the site is steep, and the outcrop on which the site is located was accessible in only one location. "Thus the aboriginal inhabitants had located themselves in an excellent position for defense" (1938:22). A second, similar site, called Upper Sky House (42Cb20), was located about 150 feet above Sky House on a similar table rock. Neither of the sites had been disturbed in any way. Examination of "architectural details, pottery and other artifacts by means of test diggings shows the second and higher site to have been contemporaneous with and similar to the one excavated" (1938:22).

Excavations at Sky House revealed an oval-shaped, clay-rimmed fireplace 4 feet 6 inches in diameter in the center of the structure. At a depth of 9 inches was a hard, sterile clay floor covering the bedrock. Around the fireplace were four postholes, apparently central roof supports. The cedar stumps of two posts were found embedded in the hard clay (Gillin 1938:23). Burned and uncharred roof beams were recovered, as were good quantities of roof adobe and willow stems. An adobe wall measuring 18 inches in height was observed in the southeast quadrant, and a second adobe wall was located in the same area but outside the 18-inch wall.

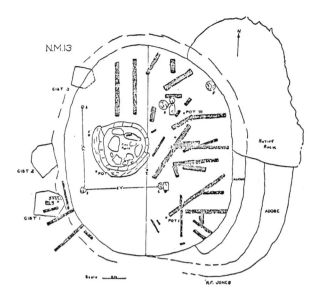

Gillin's site sketch of features at Sky House (Gillin 1938:15, Figure 7). Image courtesy of the University of Utah, Department of Anthropology.

Just outside the southwest wall, Gillin excavated a cist constructed of four stone slabs and two adobe walls. The cist, 2 feet 3 inches deep, contained a complete skeleton of a female about 30 years of age. The cranium was flattened, and the skeleton was in a flexed position with its head to the northeast. Gillin believed the body had been buried shortly before Sky House itself had burned; a burning beam had fallen just above the body's right knee, from which it was separated at the time of excavation by less than an inch of earth. The burning beam had charred the skin about the knee and preserved the tissue (1938:24).

> Beneath it was a layer composed of corncobs, squash rinds and seeds, willows, adobe balls, one stone ball, a rectangular slab of sandstone, and the broken piece of two clay figurine-like objects. The body had originally been wrapped in a rabbit-skin blanket, the few remaining strings of which completely fell apart after excavation. No pottery was found with the burial [1938:24].

A second cist was discovered directly north of the first; it was constructed of five slabs and also incorporated the back wall of Sky House. Four manos, one stone ball, and animal bones were found in the cist. A third cist was located just north of the second, constructed of five slab stones; it contained only animal bones (Gillin 1938:25). The animal bones were examined by Stephen D. Durrant of the University of Utah, who

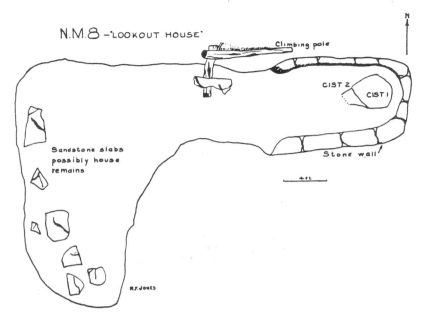

Sketch plan of site N. M. 8 (Lookout House).

identified them as bobcat, rabbit, deer, grouse, marmot, bison, mink, and squirrel (1938:29).

The most unusual artifact was a limestone figurine (limestone is, at best, extremely rare in Nine Mile Canyon):

> The piece is quite symmetrical and in shape represents a long oval constricted in the middle. On the upper portion have been incised two slanting eyebrows. Below them, each eye is indicated by an incised round hole made by a drill point. Two slanting, incised lines run off diagonally outward and downward from each eye. A nose or mouth hole, below the eyes and in the center line, seems to indicate either the one or the other anatomical feature. Three roughly parallel lines have been incised horizontally across the front of the figurine [1938:29].

Sky House was similar to other sites described (but not excavated) by Gillin in the same area. Lookout House, for example, was located on a high saddle on the north side of Nine Mile Canyon near the Ellis Ranch. The stone walls averaged 3 feet 8 inches high and enclosed an oval area about 13 feet long and 6 feet wide. Gillin believed the site was used

Scene apparently depicting warriors in combat at Warrior Ridge (42Dc1), first investigated by Gillin in 1936. Photo by Ray Boren.

primarily as a lookout or residence in times of invasion (1938:31–32). About three miles east of Sky House, Gillin noted another site (42Dc1) similar to Sky House on an elevated ridge at least 500 feet above the valley floor. Petroglyphs there depicted shield figures in costumes and shooting at one another with arrows (1938:30); this site is today referred to as Warrior Ridge, one of the most iconic sites in the canyon.

In Gillin's Footsteps

In 2010, the Colorado Plateau Archaeological Alliance used Gillin's monograph and field notes to retrace and redocument cultural features along Warrior Ridge, a remarkable assemblage of more than 90 rock art panels, residential structures, granaries, and other features that extend from the valley floor to almost 600 feet above it (Spangler 2011a). Structures on pinnacle tops have commanding views up and down the canyon (the ridge line where Sky House is located is visible to the west). In dozens of rock art "warrior" scenes, individuals are wielding clubs and spears and shooting at one another with arrows.

Gillin was struck by the similarities between Warrior Ridge (he called it NM 28) and Sky House, about three miles to the west, including the presence of adobe walls (these are no longer evident at Warrior Ridge). He observed that "the similarities in situation and culture to Sky House are apparent, although, on the surface, the NM 28 structures seemed to have suffered more deterioration, and the presence of the round, dry masonry structures of the type found at the Lookout House sites, add differences in detail" (Gillin 1938:23–24).

Gillin described Warrior Ridge as follows:

> Here was another long elevated ridge, at least 500 feet at its highest point, protruding into the main canyon in a northeast-southwest direction; this ridge forms the divide between the main canyon and a small, deep tributary entering from the south. This site has been designated NM 28. The highest point is a butte of sandstone protruding above the general level of the ridge. Here was found a quantity of gray pottery on the surface, of A and B types, a Utah-type metate, part of a broken bevel-bottomed mano, and what appeared to be the remains of a circular adobe wall. Black soil six inches deep covered the site, with sandy clay and native rock below that depth. A quantity of small charcoal was present in the soil, but no large beams. Two sets of petroglyphs on the south face of the butte showed men with tailed costumes and single-feather headdresses and with shields in their hands, shooting at each other with bows and arrows, and throwing spears at each other [1938:23].

The exact location where Gillin made these observations cannot be determined from the available description, but he was probably in the area below the pinnacle top at the far western (upper) extremity of the site. His mention of the Utah-type metate could be a reference to one of two portable metates observed here. No remnants of an adobe wall were observed in this area in 2010, and no charcoal was evident on the surface. Charcoal was observed to the southwest along the base of an outcrop, although it is likely eroding from the structures on top of the pinnacle. It does not appear that Gillin's party ventured onto the pinnacle top, as there is no mention of the circular stone structures and attached slab-lined cist at that location.

Gillin continued to the east, noting:

> Following the ridge to the east, we came upon a circular stone structure at the point of the ridge several hundred feet east from the butte

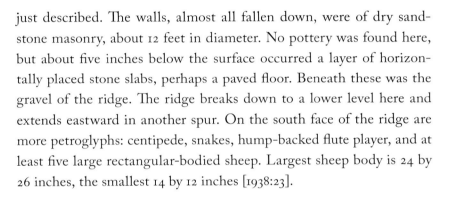

LEFT, This large masonry structure on Warrior Ridge is likely one that was first described by Gillin in 1936. Photo courtesy of the Colorado Plateau Archaeological Alliance, Ogden, Utah.

RIGHT, One of two large grinding stones found near the western edge of Warrior Ridge. Gillin (1938) mentions the presence of grinding stones in this area. Photo by Ray Boren.

just described. The walls, almost all fallen down, were of dry sandstone masonry, about 12 feet in diameter. No pottery was found here, but about five inches below the surface occurred a layer of horizontally placed stone slabs, perhaps a paved floor. Beneath these was the gravel of the ridge. The ridge breaks down to a lower level here and extends eastward in another spur. On the south face of the ridge are more petroglyphs: centipede, snakes, hump-backed flute player, and at least five large rectangular-bodied sheep. Largest sheep body is 24 by 26 inches, the smallest 14 by 12 inches [1938:23].

This structure was reidentified in 2010 as a large circular structure without associated artifacts located on a small butte about halfway down Warrior Ridge and above the series of rock art panels that face due south. The mention of large rectangular-bodied sheep is probably a reference to the four large quadrupeds and single large quadruped at the largest rock art panel here. These panels are located on the cliff face directly below the structure. The party then proceeded east:

Going still further east from the round stone structure just described, we crossed a saddle between this and the next rock outcrop. On the saddle were the ruined stone walls of three round structures, ranging from 15 to 20 feet in diameter. Test pits showed no charcoal, but merely a coating of dirt averaging 6 inches in thickness, above the native rock and gravel. Pottery: corrugated, Type C; black-on-white, Type N; and smooth gray, Type A. On the butte to the east of this saddle

RIGHT, Gillin mentioned this rock art panel, which is next to a large panel with a fifth large animal, perhaps a bighorn sheep. Photo by Ray Boren.

BELOW, This major panel on Warrior Ridge attracted Gillin's attention in 1938. Photo by Ray Boren.

was located what appeared to be another adobe-walled site. Test pits revealed small charcoal in a layer of five inches of dirt, and a collection of smooth gray pottery [Gillin 1938:23].

Gillin was undoubtedly referring to the series of circular structures along the easternmost portion of Warrior Ridge, although there is some confusion in the description. He implies there are four structures, three on the saddle and one on the pinnacle top. In reality, there are two on the saddle and one large two-room structure on the pinnacle top. This latter structure exhibits a dry-laid masonry wall around the edge of the pinnacle top and vertical wall stones on the interior, none of which are mentioned by Gillin. There are no traces of adobe walls remaining at this feature.

Gillin continued to the east: "Descending the final spur of the ridge toward the northeast, we came upon a small circular house site with what appears to be a stone paved floor and a circular wall of dry, fallen masonry. Some more smooth gray pottery, Type A, occurred here" (1938:23). This is consistent with the small circular structure located just east of the lower pinnacle. Grayware pottery is still evident at this feature.

Gillin's observations offer some insight into the rate of degradation of the features along Warrior Ridge. There are two specific references to adobe walls that are no longer evident. And the slight depressions evident at three of the eastern structures could actually be remnants of Gillin's test pits, not looters' pits. These pits have mostly deflated and revegetated, suggesting that the deflation is almost complete after about 75 years.

Tree-Ring Dating

Gillin, like other researchers before him, was hampered by a fundamental inability to place the Nine Mile Canyon sites into temporal context. How old were Valley Village and Sky House? Were they older or younger than others nearby or far distant? Various techniques had been developed throughout the Southwest that shed light on such questions—changes in house construction styles or differences in pottery from one level to another—but these were inexact methods and notoriously unreliable from region to region. A new technique developed in the 1930s would change all that: the measurement of the width of tree rings, which varied from year to year depending on the amount of moisture. Scientists at the University of Arizona were creating an index of tree rings that extended centuries into the past. When wooden beams were recovered at archaeological sites, the ancient tree rings could be compared with the index, and the approximate date the beam was cut—and hence the date the structure was built—could be established with some certainty.

Gillin knew about the new dating technology, and he was eager to apply it to the numerous portions of charred beams he had recovered from Valley Village and Sky House. But Emil Haury at the University of Arizona was unable to match the ring patterns to any established series (Gillin 1938:33) because the tree-ring index was not yet sufficiently developed. The samples were stored away but not forgotten. Edmund Schulman visited the Nine Mile Canyon area in the summer of 1946. He took samples from several pinyon pines located two miles north of Sunnyside, near the junction of Whitmore and Bear Canyons. One large pinyon at the 7,200-foot level exhibited more than 800 growth rings. However, the sample was considered undatable because of erratic growth patterns and crowded rings. In May 1948, Schulman cut down the tree and subsequently dated the core to AD 975. The sample "exceeded the previous record age for either pinyon or Rocky Mountain Douglas fir by over 100 years" (1948:4).

Schulman also examined living Douglas firs from three different areas in Nine Mile Canyon. Eight trees were sampled at an elevation of 6,500 feet just east of the confluence of Minnie Maud and Argyle Creeks. The cores dated from AD 1221 to 1550 (1948:2). Five additional trees at an elevation of 7,000 feet revealed cores that dated from AD 1236 to 1520. Ten miles west and south at an elevation of 7,300 feet, six additional samples yielded

Nine Mile Creek winds its way from west to east toward the Green River. Photo by Ray Boren.

core dates ranging from AD 1186 to 1273. Despite the combination of small annual growth and fair-to-high sensitivity, most showed few or no locally absent rings. Some samples exhibited complete records of more than 600 years. False rings were almost nonexistent, a factor attributed to lower winter temperatures and shorter growing seasons than in southern Arizona (1948:3).

Schulman also sampled Douglas firs in Indian Canyon, about 20 miles northwest of Sunnyside, and in Willow Creek, on the East Tavaputs Plateau. Both sites exhibited "essentially the same chronology." A comparison with the pinyon samples from Sunnyside showed "no important differences in chronology from the record in Douglas fir" (1948:3). Also, a detailed examination of one sample revealed an exact match with the northern Arizona tree-ring index in the fifth and sixth centuries (1948:13). Schulman concluded that "there is about as much general variation in chronology between Mesa Verde and Nine Mile some 200 miles to the north-northwest as between Mesa Verde and southern Arizona some 350 miles to the south-southwest" (1948:14).

With the index established, Schulman recovered numerous cultural wood samples from earlier archaeological expeditions into the area. In 1946, he obtained sections from six Douglas firs recovered by Gillin (1938). In 1947, Schulman visited Sky House and recovered two more samples. From the Laboratory of Anthropology at Santa Fe, Schulman obtained more than 100 small charcoal fragments collected by Reagan from four different beams from Long Mesa Ruin (42Un120) in Hill Creek Canyon on the East Tavaputs Plateau. And a single specimen from the Claflin-Emerson Expedition was obtained from Harvard University through the cooperation of John Otis Brew and Donald Scott (1948:4–5).

The initial tree-ring dates from cultural sites revealed a surprisingly narrow prehistoric occupation of both Nine Mile and Hill Creek Canyons. "It would appear that ruins in Nine Mile Canyon carried construction dates in the 950s, 1060s and 1150s; Long Mesa Ruin showed building activity later than AD 1073" (Schulman 1948:14). Seven additional tree-ring dates from Nine Mile Canyon sites were later reported, with outer ring dates ranging from AD 930 to 1089 (Ferguson 1949:1). These dates were all from Sky House (42Cb1).

Additional samples from Gillin's excavations were examined by Schulman, as were two more samples from the East Tavaputs Plateau. The Upper Sky House sample (Schulman 1951:28) was donated by the University of Utah. The Four-Name House sample was from a circular structure in a shallow cave in a cliff about 3 miles downstream from the Nutter Ranch. The site was inaccessible without ladders, although it had been entered in historic times, for the names Frank, John, Fred, and Jack had been etched on the back wall. All but one of the logs on the talus slope below the site proved to be modern poles apparently used to aid entry to the site. The Olger Ranch Ruin sample was recovered 1.5 miles down-canyon from Sky House and 5 miles above Four-Name House on the south wall of the canyon, about 200 yards south of the ranch house.

The tree-ring dates from Nine Mile and Hill Creek Canyons are not universally accepted. Smiley (1951) considered only the dating of Sky House to be "good." This site yielded three dates between AD 1055 and 1061 and six dates between AD 1078 and 1090; however, all specimens had missing rings. All the dates pointed toward a very narrowly defined Fremont presence. Gunnerson (1960) and Ambler (1969) reexamined the research of Schulman (1948, 1950, 1951, 1954) and Smiley (1951) and compared the tree-ring data with evidence of well-dated Ancestral Puebloan ceramics found in Fremont contexts. Gunnerson concluded that "it seems advisable to date the Fremont culture at about AD 950 to 1200, for the best tree-ring dates fall for the most part in that period, and dates before about AD 1000 are questionable. Moreover, the trade pottery supports an AD 950–1200 range for Fremont sites in the middle and southern parts of the area" (1960:376).

Gunnerson's conclusion, one embraced by other researchers at the time, was erroneous only in that he applied the Nine Mile tree-ring data to a

Warrior scenes so common at Warrior Ridge are rare elsewhere in Nine Mile Canyon. Photo by Ray Boren.

much broader area instead of limiting it to Nine Mile Canyon specifically. Subsequent research in Nine Mile Canyon, as well as in neighboring Desolation Canyon and Range Creek, has produced a large number of radiocarbon dates that support the contention that the entire West Tavaputs Plateau was the focus of a very intense agricultural occupation from about AD 950 to 1200, with most of the dates falling at AD 1000 to 1050 (Spangler and Jones 2009; Duncan Metcalfe, personal communication, 2011; see also Chapter 7). Was the area occupied before and after that time? Certainly it was, but the evidence is sparse when compared with the overwhelming number of tree-ring dates and radiocarbon dates between AD 950 and 1200.

After Nine Mile

On leaving Nine Mile Canyon, Gillin immediately wrote to Scott that he hoped to have a report written later that fall, indicating, "As soon as I get the report finished...I shall send it along to you and hope I can impose upon you to criticize it" (1936e). A draft of the manuscript was later sent to Scott, and Gillin acknowledges both Scott and Brew for reading the monograph and offering their helpful criticisms. What isn't mentioned is that the manuscript Gillin prepared was not the one that was eventually published. The original manuscript, titled "Archaeological Investigations in Nine Mile Canyon, with Notes on a Site near Nephi," included an entire section on Gillin's Nephi excavations, along with photographic plates. The section on the Nephi mounds was subsequently dropped, and given the high cost of reproducing the photographs, at least 24 were eliminated, including all the Nephi photos and presumably some of the Nine Mile Canyon photos (Gillin 1937c). The Nine Mile photographs are currently lost from the University of Utah collections.

Shortly after his return from Nine Mile Canyon, Gillin began laying the groundwork for a summer expedition to central Utah. Unlike the cash-strapped Nine Mile expedition, this project was to be a well-funded joint endeavor between the University of Utah and Donald Scott and the Peabody Museum. In the spring of 1937, the Board of Regents approved the partnership, which, according to an April 2, 1937, letter from Gillin to President Thomas, committed the University of Utah to fund $500 in field costs and $400 toward Gillin's salary; the Peabody Museum would pay $500 toward field costs, the costs of a Peabody Museum archaeologist, Donald Scott's travel costs, and the costs of publishing the monograph (Gillin 1937d).

The university approved the partnership despite the fact that Gillin had by that time submitted his resignation, indicating that he had accepted a teaching position at Ohio State University. Minutes of the Board of Regents meeting note that the resignation was effective June 30 of that year (Board of Regents 1937), but a letter to Gillin from President Thomas approved Gillin's request to remain on the university payroll through September 1 (Thomas 1937), presumably to allow completion of the 1937 central Utah investigations.

The 1937 expedition featured one Peabody Museum representative, John M. Longyear; Gillin represented the University of Utah, along with eight students, including Robert Lister, William Mulloy, and Carling Malouf, all of whom would go on to stellar careers in archaeology. The expedition was far-ranging, from the Richfield area on the south to Tooele on the north, with a particular focus on residential sites in the Marysvale, Ephraim, and Tooele areas. In an ironic twist on Gillin's earlier admonition that field notes and at least 50 percent of the collections be deposited at the University Museum, these regulations were apparently not followed in this instance. Photographs and collections from the 1937 expedition are now housed at the Peabody Museum, but the location of Gillin's field notes is unknown.

Gillin's reasons for leaving the University of Utah after a brief two-year stint are not stated in any of the correspondence, but it can be implied from

One of Gillin's many photographs from his "Central Utah" investigations, now catalogued at the Peabody Museum. His Nine Mile photographs have been lost. Photo (No. 133380047) courtesy of the Peabody Museum of Archaeology and Ethnology, Harvard University.

his letters (1936e) that he was homesick and longed for collegial interaction with fellow anthropologists. His academic interests were still rooted in anthropology, and nothing in Utah seems to have caught his attention. According to the biographical sketch compiled by the Peabody Museum, he stayed at Ohio State University from 1937 until 1941, during which time he also spent a year at Yale University's Institute of Human Relations, where he studied the intersection of psychology and anthropology. In 1942, Gillin accepted a position in the Anthropology Department at Duke University, but with the onset of World War II he was assigned to the U.S. Embassy in Lima, Peru. Gillin continued to teach at Duke until 1946, when he accepted a professorship at the University of North Carolina in Chapel Hill, where he founded the anthropology Ph.D. program. He left North Carolina in 1959 to found the Department of Anthropology at the University of Pittsburgh, from which he retired in 1972. He died the following year (Harvard University Library 1998).

Gillin's tenure at the University of Utah, albeit brief, marked a beginning and an end, both of them relevant to Nine Mile Canyon. It was the beginning of formal archaeological research conducted within the context of sound science and rigorous academic standards, a development that would be enhanced by the arrival of Jesse D. Jennings at the university a decade later. And it marked the end of the "Crimson Cowboy" era—the Peabody Museum's 10-year interest in Utah archaeology north of the Colorado River. And in some respects, it also marked the end of the University of Utah's interest in Nine Mile Canyon. Almost four decades would pass before university scholars would again focus their attention on Nine Mile Canyon, and when they did, this generation hailed from Brigham Young University.

6

Rock Art, Settlement Patterns, and a Broader Understanding of Nine Mile Canyon

As regards the Nine Mile culture in general, a number of inconsistencies are noticeable. House types, pottery and stone work fail to fall into the classical complexes. —JOHN GILLIN (1938:29)

A Wider View: The First Large-Scale Surveys

The publication of John Gillin's *Archaeological Investigations in Nine Mile Canyon, Utah (During the Year 1936)* first brought Nine Mile Canyon's rich and perplexing archaeological resources to the attention of the archaeological world. And it could have been—should have been—the impetus for a new generation of archaeologists to follow in his footsteps, exploring the many questions raised by Gillin's work. The questions are myriad: Are Valley Village and Sky House truly representative of settlement patterns in the canyon as a whole or are they anomalies? Do they represent occupations at the same point in time by identical groups of people? Or did the ancients once live on the valley floor next to fields and water, only to shift to defensible positions high above the valley floor in response to a perceived threat? What was this threat? Were these groups really Fremont farmers akin to those living in the San Rafael Swell and Uinta Basin, or were they immigrants from distant regions bringing with them new ideas and approaches to farming in harsh climates? Most fundamental, when did these events occur?

But such academic interest in Nine Mile Canyon never really materialized, and the region was largely ignored by university scholars for much of the next half century. There was an occasional mention or two of the canyon in professional publications, but there was no serious sequel to Gillin's groundbreaking research (1938). And documentation of the canyon's abundant resources eventually fell to groups of concerned university students and dedicated amateurs whose efforts were driven more by passion for protecting the canyon than interest in addressing basic questions related to human behavior.

The reasons behind the intellectual snub are likely many. After Gillin's departure from the University of Utah in 1937, the university's

OPPOSITE, Bighorn sheep with long, sweeping horns are the most common animal depicted in Nine Mile Canyon rock art. Photo by Ray Boren.

anthropology program lacked any clear theoretical direction or decisive mission (Janetski 1997). Not only was Nine Mile Canyon ignored, but there was little university research being conducted anywhere else in the state. And what scant research was done never rose to the level of prestigious monographs or public attention. Archaeological research virtually ceased with the outbreak of World War II, when many young scholars gave up their trowels and shovels for rifles and bayonets. Some of them never returned.

The arrival of Jesse D. Jennings at the university in 1948 was a watershed moment for Utah archaeology; over his thirty-year tenure there, Jennings restored the university's reputation as a premier research entity of national renown. But Jennings was never much interested in Nine Mile Canyon, preferring instead to direct his remarkable organizational skills toward the establishment of broad but essential frameworks for Utah cultural history—a foundation that remains the backbone of current research in Utah. In the process, Jennings synthesized huge quantities of archaeological data into readable and publicly accessible reports. In 1953, he established the Great Basin Archaeological Conference and expanded the Museum of Anthropology into the Utah Museum of Natural History (Spangler 2002).

The Utah Statewide Archeological Survey

Jennings's organizational skills made him perfectly suited to tackle a wide range of geographically massive projects, all geared toward "big picture" syntheses of vast quantities of regional data. Shortly after his arrival at the University of Utah, Jennings initiated a systematic survey of the entire state to document archaeological resources, most of which had been earlier ignored in favor of large and spectacular sites. Begun in 1949, the surveys were intended to be a ten-year effort that would also serve to train graduate students through field research programs (Gunnerson 1959). In 1951, the project was modified "to give it greater continuity," and it was assigned the title of the Utah Statewide Archeological Survey. The stated intent of the survey was to (1) systematically survey, record, and collect from as many sites as possible; (2) conduct limited test excavations at significant sites; (3) analyze and report the findings of the survey; and (4) salvage archaeological data from sites threatened by destruction. The state was divided into five sections, each to be the subject of a separate report (Rudy 1953:ix).

Evolving priorities hampered the "statewide" surveys—in particular the need to salvage archaeological data from the Green River and Colorado River corridors before they were inundated by the Flaming Gorge and Glen Canyon Dams—and large portions of the state were never investigated. Eventually, the Utah Statewide Archeological Survey evolved into a salvage archaeology program that initiated investigations on behalf of the Utah State Road Commission, U.S. Forest Service, Utah State Park Commission, and National Park Service (Gunnerson 1959). In the late 1950s, the survey coexisted with the massive Upper Colorado River Basin Salvage Program, and the survey's objectives were subsumed within the larger Glen Canyon project (Jennings 1959).

The statewide survey began with work around Virgin City and Gunlock in southwestern Utah in anticipation of the construction of two reservoirs there (Gunnerson 1959; Rudy and Stirland 1950). The Gunlock area was where Gillin had intended to investigate before he retreated "sulkily" to Nine Mile Canyon in 1936. From 1950 to 1952, survey director Jack R. Rudy led a series of surveys in northwestern, western, and southwestern Utah as far south as Iron County and as far north as Box Elder County (Rudy 1953, 1954). In 1952, the survey again shifted priorities, this time to southeastern Utah, where road construction in the Beef Basin area had resulted in rampant vandalism (Gunnerson 1959; Rudy 1955).

The statewide survey generated three major publications (Gunnerson 1957; Rudy 1953; Rudy and Stirland 1950), but only Gunnerson's *Archeological Survey of the Fremont Area* deals with the Tavaputs Plateau region. This survey was initiated to "place site data on record, to formulate limited generalizations concerning the Fremont Culture" (Gunnerson 1957:1), and to obtain a "better knowledge of the distribution of the Fremont culture and…its variations in its later phases" (1957:4). The objective was to visit as many sites as possible and make surface collections. Gunnerson's reconnaissance, carried out during July, August, and September 1954, was restricted to areas that could be reached by pickup truck (Gunnerson 1955:1).

The Owl Panel in middle Nine Mile Canyon. Photo by Ray Boren.

Gunnerson's primary emphasis was sites having ceramic materials and other diagnostic artifacts. Sites were assigned to the Fremont culture chiefly on the basis of pottery, and a second group was classified as tentatively Fremont based on architecture, rock art, or circumstantial evidence. According to Gunnerson, the survey provided information concerning the geographic limits of the Fremont culture, evidence for population density, and data on the range of variation of Fremont culture traits (1957:4).

Gunnerson concluded that Fremont villages were never large but were frequently close together. Dwelling structures were typically found in groups of fewer than five rooms, usually independent of one another (Gunnerson 1957:4–5). Dwellings were generally semi-subterranean open structures or surface structures inside rockshelters (1957:5–7). The predominantly gray ceramics were almost all tempered with either calcite or basalt (1957:9), and projectile points were predominantly triangular and less than 3 centimeters long (1957:25).

Gunnerson's synthesis of the cultural data often lacked specificity and failed to adequately describe Fremont population dynamics, regional variability, or complexity. The survey also lacked any systematic or statistical approach to site distribution, and the primarily descriptive report exhibited a fundamental bias toward well-known and easily accessible sites, appearing to contradict Gunnerson's stated intent to survey the "least known" areas of Utah (1957:i).

Nine Mile Canyon played a very minor role in Gunnerson's synthesis, and he offered no real explanation as to why he gave the canyon such short

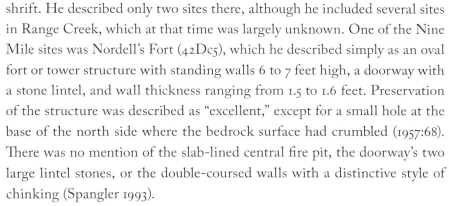

shrift. He described only two sites there, although he included several sites in Range Creek, which at that time was largely unknown. One of the Nine Mile sites was Nordell's Fort (42Dc5), which he described simply as an oval fort or tower structure with standing walls 6 to 7 feet high, a doorway with a stone lintel, and wall thickness ranging from 1.5 to 1.6 feet. Preservation of the structure was described as "excellent," except for a small hole at the base of the north side where the bedrock surface had crumbled (1957:68). There was no mention of the slab-lined central fire pit, the doorway's two large lintel stones, or the double-coursed walls with a distinctive style of chinking (Spangler 1993).

The other Nine Mile Canyon site (42Dc6) was located about 0.6 miles west of the Gate Canyon confluence, situated on a rock outcrop about 85 feet above the valley floor. Gunnerson described the remains of several dry-laid masonry walls, one with an oval base about 10 feet by 15 feet. Other structures were largely indistinguishable (1957:68). This site is probably Pete's Village, located on a prominent outcrop at the mouth of Petes Canyon. Although his foray into Nine Mile Canyon was apparently brief, Gunnerson would later make one of the most important contributions to the archaeology of the canyon. He left the University of Utah to complete a Ph.D. at Harvard University, where his dissertation included editing and publishing the long-lost notes from the Claflin-Emerson Expedition, including those from the 1931 exploration of Nine Mile Canyon and the Tavaputs Plateau (Gunnerson 1969).

Elaborate rock art panels are found at every cliff level in Nine Mile Canyon to almost 1,000 feet above the valley floor. Photo by Ray Boren.

Rasmussen Cave Revisited

Despite its rather ostentatious title of "The Archaeological and Historical Research Committee of the University of Santa Clara, California," this research project, directed by Francis R. Flaim and Austen D. Warburton, could be classified as an expedition led by amateur archaeologists. Flaim, a university botany professor, organized the expedition in 1959 for a group of interested university students for the purpose of archaeological survey and excavations. A published report (Flaim and Warburton 1961) made reference to fieldwork from 1954 to 1959, although the excavations and student involvement occurred only in 1959 (Francis Flaim, personal communication 1991). Research from 1954 through 1958 was apparently confined to informal survey, and in 1959, efforts were focused exclusively on excavations at Rasmussen Cave (42Cb16), at that time owned by Humbert Pressett (Flaim and Warburton 1961:19).

These "excavations" involved sifting refuse from excavations made three decades before by Donald Scott (1931a), Noel Morss (1931a), and various looters. Among the items recovered were several slate beads, numerous corncobs, dent corn, bone fragments, a bone awl, molded clay fragments, a flint knife, and a 3-inch-long rectangular stone object painted transversely with five red lines and traces of black pigment. The only pottery reported was a single fragment of thick grayware (Flaim and Warburton 1961:20–21). Also reported was a short corncob figurine, approximately 5 inches in length, with its head flaring to a width of 2 inches. The figurine had eyes and body markings that had been burned onto the cob (1961:23). The report also described five unfired clay figurines and five partial figurines found at the rear of the cave.

Flaim and Warburton made reference to ongoing research and future reports (1961:23), but no such reports were ever produced (Francis Flaim, personal communication 1991). No archaeological field notes were kept, and photographs were not taken in any systematic order. The location of most artifacts and field photographs is unknown, although some were in Flaim's personal possession in 1991, and others, including the remains of an infant strapped to a cradleboard, were donated to the Prehistoric Museum at the College of Eastern Utah in Price (Flaim 1961). Flaim was uncertain which artifacts were recovered during the Santa Clara project and which were collected during his own recreational excursions into Nine Mile Canyon.

Making Order of Rock Art

Perhaps no single person has defined Utah rock art research more than Polly Schaafsma, whose work on the topic began with a report for the University of Utah in 1970, followed by her classic monograph *Rock Art of Utah* (1971) for Harvard's Peabody Museum. The monograph, since reprinted, continues to be the most frequently cited report describing Utah rock art styles and chronologies.

Schaafsma's first attempt to define Utah rock art came with the unpublished "Survey Report of the Rock Art of Utah," in which she attempted to "locate the outstanding sites and to relate them to the known archeology of the region" (1970:1). Relevant to Nine Mile Canyon, the report mentions the well-known Great Hunt Panel in Cottonwood Canyon (Schaafsma 1970:28), the abundant and unusual rock art found inside Rasmussen Cave (42Cb16) (1970:61), a panel in middle Nine Mile Canyon characterized by naturalistic figures and horned trapezoidal anthropomorphs (1970:63–64),

"Shield figures" are common in Nine Mile Canyon. Photo courtesy of the Colorado Plateau Archaeological Alliance, Ogden, Utah.

and the enigmatic Sheep Canyon pictographs, which reflect both Barrier Canyon and Fremont styles (1970:84–85).

Schaafsma's subsequent report for the Peabody Museum was based almost entirely on photographs made by previous researchers, primarily the Donald Scott Collection but also photographs from the Reagan and Beckwith expeditions. From this database, Schaafsma identified a Fremont style in the Tavaputs Plateau area that she labeled "San Rafael Fremont: Northern Zone" (1971:28), a term that is still the preferred nomenclature.

The dominant motif in all Fremont rock art is unquestionably the distinctive trapezoidal anthropomorph. However, from region to region these anthropomorphs exhibit considerable variability in size, shape, internal features, and appendages. Generally, Fremont anthropomorphs have broad shoulders. These figures often exhibit elaborate headdresses (horns, antlers, antennae-like projectiles, feathers, fringes), jewelry, and clothing. Hair bobs similar to those observed on Basketmaker figures are common in northeastern Utah and northwestern Colorado. Facial decorations are frequently shown, suggesting the depiction of masks (Schaafsma 1971; see also Cole 1990).

Typical "Northern Zone" anthropomorphs found in Nine Mile Canyon. Photo courtesy of the Colorado Plateau Archaeological Alliance, Ogden, Utah.

Schaafsma suggested that the San Rafael Fremont: Northern Zone "petroglyphs and rock paintings…exhibit a stylistic phase of Fremont rock art which is internally consistent and distinct from that of the Uinta region and which can be differentiated from that of the southern San Rafael zone" (1971:28–29). In particular, the Northern San Rafael Style prevalent in Nine Mile Canyon lacked the large, precisely executed trapezoidal anthropomorphs and shield bearers with detailed ornamentation commonly found in the Vernal area. Instead, the panels were crowded with small, solidly pecked figures, often carelessly executed and ill-defined (1971:29).

According to Schaafsma's analysis, Northern Zone anthropomorphs exhibit a typological norm of a trapezoidal body and bucket-shaped head. The body form may be flared at the base to suggest a kilt, and some anthropomorphs were portrayed with long, rake-like horns or antlers. These figures have arms, which are commonly bent at the elbow, and hands with spread fingers. Legs are usually short and straight. Some anthropomorphs display rectangular or triangular body shapes instead of the usual trapezoidal configuration. The majority of anthropomorphs, regardless of size, are solidly painted or pecked (1971:29–31).

A predictable weakness in Schaafsma's research stemmed from her raw data, which were inherently biased toward large or aesthetically pleasing sites that had drawn the attention of photographers over the years. She made no attempt to catalog all rock art sites in any given area, and she had no idea whether these large panels were in fact a valid sample of the thousands of rock art panels that are present in Nine Mile Canyon alone. Certain

Typical "horned snake" figure in Nine Mile Canyon. Photo by Jerry D. Spangler.

elements Schaafsma dismissed as not present are, in fact, present, often in significant numbers. For example, she claimed there were no examples in the Northern Zone of foot exaggeration, a common characteristic of Uinta Basin anthropomorphs (1971:29). In fact, this motif is a frequently seen anthropomorphic element in the Tavaputs Plateau, particularly in lower Nine Mile Canyon (Spangler 1993).

Also, Schaafsma claimed that the hump-backed flute player motif was nonexistent in the Nine Mile Canyon region. Actually, this motif has been observed throughout Nine Mile Canyon (Gillin 1938:30; Reagan 1933a:62–63; Strevell and Pulver 1935:17; Spangler 2011a). In yet another example, Schaafsma noted only 13 serpent representations in the entire northern zone, five of which had horns or plumes (1971:36). Many intensive surveys in middle and lower Nine Mile Canyon since 1991 have revealed that snake-like figures, more often with horn-like representations than without, are the second-most common zoomorph reflected in Nine Mile Canyon rock art, numbering well in excess of two hundred such images (Spangler 1993, 2008, 2009, 2011a, 2011b).

More recent large-scale surveys of Nine Mile Canyon rock art have also demonstrated that the classic Fremont anthropomorph—the human figure with broad shoulders tapering to a narrower waist—is actually surprisingly rare. In fact, it represents a very minor portion of all anthropomorphs depicted (less than 10 percent). The reality is that Nine Mile Canyon anthropomorphs come in every imaginable shape: round, oval, cigar-shaped, square, rectangular, amorphous, trapezoidal, and even combinations of shapes. Some are imposingly large (greater than 1 meter in height), and others are tiny (less than 5 centimeters in height). In short, when the entire catalog of images is considered, it begs the question whether the images are even Fremont rock art, at least as Schaafsma defined it.

Nevertheless, Schaafsma's efforts should be lauded, not for the fundamental weaknesses in her approach (e.g., her small sample of sites) but for her attempts to create order amid the chaos that defined rock art studies throughout the state at that time. Rather than speculate endlessly as to the meaning of rock art, she reviewed raw data and offered up a hypothesis, thereby inviting other scholars to test its validity. Few have taken on that challenge.

Typical "Fremont" figure in Nine Mile Canyon. Notice the small Fremont figure inside the large one in bas-relief. Photo courtesy of the Colorado Plateau Archaeological Alliance, Ogden, Utah.

Can Rock Art Speak?

Archaeologists are notoriously reticent to study rock art. Most of those who choose to work in the Nine Mile Canyon region are understandably awestruck by the sheer quantity of images, and in some cases at the remarkable skills and fearlessness of the ancient artists, whose images can be found high on cliffs and along the narrowest of ledges. But a fundamental goal of archaeology is to explain human behavior, and therein is the problem: How do you construct a sound, testable scientific hypothesis related to rock art when we in the twenty-first century have no clue as to the ancients' world view? Rock art is generally viewed as a symbolic representation of ideas. But what and whose ideas are represented? Is it representative of actual events? Is it a manifestation of the abstract—of religion, cosmology, and belief systems? All these concepts are ones that archaeologists find difficult to address within the constructs of scientific methods. In many respects, rock art is commonly viewed as background noise, a distraction to scholars who grapple with broader behavioral questions like human responses to changing climates.

The irony is that rock art—and Nine Mile Canyon has more of it than any other place in Utah—represents visible, tangible evidence of what is otherwise intangible. And as such the canyon represents an ideal outdoor laboratory where rock art can be studied within the context of sound science

Rams, ewes, and lambs at the Great Hunt Panel. Photo by Ray Boren.

(respected archaeologists elsewhere in the Southwest are embracing new theoretical approaches to rock art studies with exciting potential; see, for example, Geib 1996, Hayden 1998, Robins 1997 and 2002, and Robins and Hays-Gilpin 2000). A key element to these studies is statistical analysis of spatial distribution of rock art sites and certain diagnostic images, and their relationship to topographic features and other archaeological sites. This approach—greatly accelerated today by the proliferation of global information system technology—was first attempted about 80 years ago when Julian Steward published *Petroglyphs of California and Adjoining States* (1929b), in which he plotted the geographic distribution of various motifs.

In northeastern Utah, a similar attempt was initiated in the 1980s. Years earlier, Nine Mile rock art had come to the attention of Kenneth Castleton, a medical doctor and amateur rock art enthusiast with a close personal relationship with Jesse Jennings. With Jennings's encouragement, Castleton began organizing his vast collection of Utah rock art photographs, which was eventually published by the Utah Museum of Natural History in two volumes, along with Castleton's personal observations gleaned from a lifetime of visiting Utah rock art (Castleton 1984, 1987).

Castleton noted obvious differences between Nine Mile Canyon rock art, characterized by large numbers of solidly pecked figures, and that of the Vernal area to the north, where figures were more dominating, typically pecked in outline and executed with a stylistic artistry absent in Nine Mile Canyon. Castleton described the rock art in Nine Mile Canyon as "small and often rather densely packed, with many animals, especially deer or sheep" (1984:82). He was also struck by the sheer quantity of sites, noting hundreds of panels and thousands of figures in the canyon.

Castleton's photographic catalog was also used to establish statewide geographic distributions of selected rock art elements (Castleton and Madsen 1981). When the distribution of various elements was plotted on statewide maps, several definite patterns emerged. Predictably, elements common to the Uinta Basin and Tavaputs Plateau included mountain sheep, anthropomorphs with horns or antennae, triangular anthropomorphs, bows and arrows, necklaces, facial features, and shield figures. More telling was that all the elements examined were significantly more common on the Colorado Plateau than west of the Wasatch Mountains:

> The large number of these elements and the number of sites in which they are found suggest that there was a relatively high degree of interaction north and south along the drainages of the Colorado River, and somewhat more limited interaction between the Great Basin and Southwest generally. In terms of rock art alone, a case could be made for a higher degree of interrelatedness between Anasazi [Ancestral Puebloan] and Fremont on the Colorado Plateau than could be made for interaction between the Fremont of the Great Basin and those of the Colorado Plateau [Castleton and Madsen 1981:173].

There have been a few more recent attempts to tease human behavior from the Nine Mile rock art panels. Ray Matheny and colleagues (1997) examined the Great Hunt Panel in Cottonwood Canyon and other hunting scenes in Nine Mile Canyon within the context of animal behavior. They determined that the prehistoric artists had an intimate understanding of bighorn sheep behavior. The proportion of rams, ewes, and lambs is representative of that observed in nature during the late fall or early winter when an entire herd gathers for the annual rut. Other accuracies include the isolation of rams from ewes, a hierarchical order of bighorns in procession, rams engaged in dominance behavior, and tails depicting alarm (or absence thereof). In short, "indigenous rock art of Nine Mile Canyon

Nine Mile Canyon features an abundance of images depicting individuals carrying large packs. Photo courtesy of the Colorado Plateau Archaeological Alliance, Ogden, Utah.

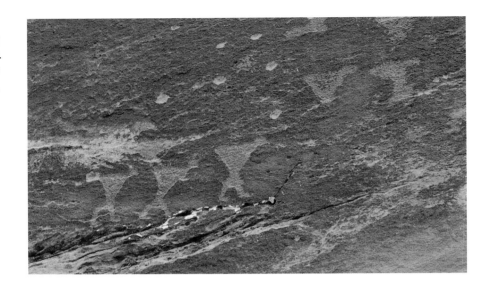

possessed structure and was not a kind of doodling or random efforts of passersby" (Matheny 2005:4).

Matheny and others also examined the distribution of images that depict humans carrying what appear to be backpacks—he calls them "burden bearers" (Matheny et al. 2004; Matheny 2005). Some 340 burden-bearer images were identified, most of them in association with hunting scenes depicting bighorn sheep. Fremont hunting scenes often show anthropomorphs with outstretched arms as if driving bighorn sheep toward archers with arrows pointed at oncoming animals; canines driving animals toward hunters; and utilization of enclosures and nets, all of which have been documented in ethnographic contexts in the Great Basin.

Matheny (2005) has further argued that the rock art of Nine Mile Canyon, dominated by hunting scenes, suggests a socioeconomic system that extended far beyond the canyon and may indicate that Fremont peoples exploited Nine Mile Canyon primarily for animal products that they exported. Systematic hunting expeditions used nets, dogs, and ambush strategies to acquire bighorn sheep, mainly during the late fall and early winter. The depiction of rows of individuals carrying large packs is indicative of human transport of procured meat, and the predominance of these figures at the mouths of side canyons that offered access to the highlands suggests trade routes by which the meat was transported to sedentary groups for winter consumption.

Organized burden bearers in Nine Mile Canyon and their association with bighorn sheep suggest a specialized quest for high-rank animals. Elk and deer and a stray bison may be fortuitous game taken during the specialized hunt for bighorn sheep. The evidence here negates the down-the-line model where trade goods moved from individual to individual as an explanation for the rock art. Instead, the evidence fits a larger trade network model not yet formulated for the Fremont involving procurement expeditions, perhaps by professional traders, and possibly by villages with controlling sociopolitical organizations [Matheny 2005:14].

This coursed masonry structure was one of only five sites with architecture described by Hurst and Louthan during their 1974–75 survey. Photo courtesy of the Colorado Plateau Archaeological Alliance, Ogden, Utah.

The Concerned Students

One significant attempt to organize and understand the rock art of Nine Mile Canyon occurred in the mid-1970s, when a group of Brigham Young

University students, worried about the deterioration and vandalism of Nine Mile Canyon rock art sites, created the Public Archaeology Research Group to conduct an intensive rock art survey along a 3.6-mile section of the canyon. The purpose of the project, conducted between March 1974 and June 1975, was to obtain a complete rock art inventory of as much of the north wall of the canyon as possible (Hurst and Louthan 1979:5). Because of the difficulty of the terrain, much of the survey was confined to lower canyon levels, while the survey of the upper levels was inconsistent at best (Winston Hurst, personal communication 1992).

The selective nature of the "intensive" survey—with its greater emphasis on the lower cliff levels, where rock art is not only more accessible but more abundant—may account for the skewed ratio of rock art sites to structure sites. Some 122 sites were recorded during the course of the survey, of which 117 were rock art sites with 325 separate panels. The five remaining sites were architectural structures of coursed masonry or slab-lined structures. A few rock art sites were also associated with architectural remains, but the rarity of architecture was especially noteworthy (Hurst and Louthan 1979:22–24).

Two distinctive site distribution patterns were noted. The density of sites decreased in proportion to the distance from the canyon bottom, and rock art tended to be clustered around the mouths of side canyons. There were exceptions to both patterns. For example, site 42Dc212 was located 700 feet above the canyon floor. Researchers also attempted to categorize the rock art style of Nine Mile Canyon by using trait and element analysis and examining the superimposition of newer images over older ones. Five styles were identified, suggesting "a greater variety of occupation periods than previously indicated" (Hurst and Louthan 1979:53–54).

Unlike previous rock art projects that focused on large or aesthetically pleasing sites, this project constituted the first attempt to consider the distribution of *all* rock art features in a defined area. Some sites were predictably large with hundreds of images. Others were small with one or two images. But the total was substantially greater than anyone had previously surmised—about 30 sites per linear mile. In 2010, roughly half of the sites described in 1974–75 were reidentified and redocumented by the Colorado Plateau Archaeological Alliance as part of an ongoing study of site degradation over time. This effort found that the 1974–75 survey had understated

One of the many sites first described by BYU students in 1974–75 and redocumented in 2010. Photo courtesy of the Colorado Plateau Archaeological Alliance, Ogden, Utah.

the number of rock art panels by about 20 percent *and* that architectural features are actually present in substantial numbers (Spangler 2011b).

The lasting legacy of the BYU students' brief foray in the canyon rests not with the scientific contribution of their monograph, the first to have been published on the archaeology of the canyon since Gillin's in 1938. Rather, the project established a template for a later, decade-long effort to comprehensively catalog all the canyon's resources. This subsequent effort was led by Pam Miller, at the time an archaeologist at the Prehistoric Museum in Price; her husband, Blaine Miller, the Bureau of Land Management archaeologist in Price; Deanne Matheny, an archaeologist and attorney; and her husband, Ray T. Matheny, an archaeology professor at Brigham Young University. The Millers and Deanne Matheny were among the "concerned students" who participated in the 1974–75 surveys. Their efforts in the 1980s and 1990s rank as probably the largest volunteer archaeological project ever undertaken in the state.

Carbon County Volunteers

In 1986, the Utah Legislature appropriated funds for the establishment of a training program for amateurs interested in preserving and recording archaeological sites. Three years later, Carbon County and the Castle Valley Chapter of the Utah Statewide Archaeological Society (USAS) applied for state historical preservation funds with the express purpose of conducting "an inventory of the cultural resources of Nine Mile Canyon" (Miller and Matheny 1990:123). The first survey, in 1989, employed 51

The Sheep Canyon pictographs were initially mentioned by Gillin and were later formally documented by Carbon County volunteers. Photo courtesy of Jerry D. Spangler.

volunteers, many of them graduates of the Utah Avocational Archaeologist Certification Program. The goals of the long-term project were to (1) provide an opportunity for amateurs to be involved in a worthwhile archaeological project, (2) determine what types of archaeological sites were represented in Nine Mile Canyon, (3) locate sites that could be used as points of interest for the increasing number of recreational visitors to the canyon, and (4) use the information from the inventory as justification for the nomination of Nine Mile Canyon to the National Register of Historic Places and possibly the World Heritage Site List (Miller and Matheny 1990:125). More than 300 sites were ultimately recorded and several radiocarbon dates were reported, all consistent with Fremont farming.

One hundred sites were recorded during the 1989 survey, which concentrated on a two-mile area of upper Nine Mile Canyon from the mouth of Argyle Canyon to the Duchesne County line, then upstream through Nine Mile Canyon to Sheep Canyon and the Rich Ranch (Matheny and Matheny 1990:6–7). This area had earlier been investigated by John Gillin (1938), and several of the sites documented by the USAS crews had been described by Gillin, including Valley Village, Beacon Ridge, and the Sheep Canyon pictographs. Two other sites, located 770 and 750 feet above the valley floor, respectively, "include several units and other features but likely were not habitations. The access to water is hundreds of vertical feet below and the sites must have had a special function in the society to warrant the expense of labor to construct and maintain them in such inconvenient places" (Matheny and Matheny 1990:23).

Volunteer crews returned in 1990 and documented an additional 79 sites in an area of middle Nine Mile Canyon approximately 1 mile long, from 0.5 miles east of Blind Canyon to the mouth of Dry Canyon. Researchers noted a marked increase in the density of sites in this area of the canyon compared with the upper canyon area surveyed in 1989. These included a greater number of small granaries tucked away in rockshelters and residential sites situated on knolls and ridges just above the floodplain. Maize from a storage structure at 42Cb615 yielded a radiocarbon date of 990 ± 70 BP (cal AD 896–1213). And maize from 42Cb667 returned a radiocarbon date of 1710 ± 80 BP (cal AD 129–537), the earliest evidence of horticulture so far documented in Nine Mile Canyon (Matheny et al. 1991).

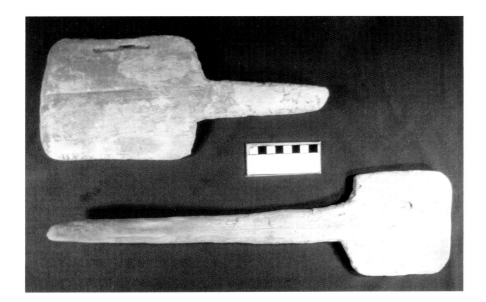

Shovel-shaped implements recovered by Carbon County volunteers in Nine Mile Canyon. Photo courtesy of Jerry D. Spangler.

Two shovel-shaped implements constructed of cottonwood were located in a camouflaged subterranean storage structure (42Cb729), and a digging stick was recovered at yet another storage facility (42Cb731) (Matheny et al. 1991:9). A portion of one cottonwood shovel from 42Cb729 was radiocarbon dated to 1100 ± 90 BP (cal AD 692–1157), and wood from a digging stick at 42Cb710 yielded a radiocarbon date of 990 ± 50 BP (cal AD 978–1162). The cottonwood shovels are virtually identical to wooden implements recovered in Douglas Creek, Colorado (Wenger 1956), by private collectors in Nine Mile Canyon (Gunnerson 1962), and in Desolation Canyon (Spangler and Jones 2009).

The 1991 Nine Mile Canyon survey began where the previous year's survey ended at Dry Canyon and proceeded east downstream a distance of less than a mile. Fifty-two sites were recorded, among them Rasmussen Cave (Matheny et al. 1992). In 1992, crews surveyed the portion of Nine Mile Canyon from the mouth of Dry Canyon to the mouth of Cottonwood Canyon. Seventy-four additional sites were recorded, and researchers recognized an emerging pattern: granaries were visible in most cases from a considerable distance, and no attempt was made to hide them, whereas small subterranean cists were intentionally concealed in "places that are difficult to access and they may not have been storage units for ordinary food items" (Matheny 1993:4).

The USAS surveys continued through 1999, but enthusiasm gradually waned. The number of volunteers dropped dramatically, and those who were still participating got older and less capable of ascending the steep slopes. Hundreds of sites were documented between 1993 and 1999, but the site forms were never completed or archived with the state, and formal reports of the later field seasons have not yet been completed. Nonetheless, the Nine Mile Canyon surveys are unique in the annals of Utah archaeology in that certified amateurs provided the field crews necessary for an intensive survey. Thousands of volunteer hours were donated, and hundreds of sites were formally recorded. And for the first time, broad areas of the canyon had been thoroughly examined, demonstrating a site density of 30 to 50 sites per mile in the upper reaches of Nine Mile Canyon and 80 to 90 per mile in the middle portion—a staggering density that rivals even that of the famed Cedar Mesa in San Juan County. More importantly, scores of sites documented by the volunteers have now been listed on the National Register of Historic Places.

Frank's Place

At the same time that Carbon County volunteers were working in middle Nine Mile Canyon under Matheny's direction, Matheny was leading a Brigham Young University field school in lower Nine Mile Canyon from 1989 to 1991. The field school, based at the historic Pace Ranch, where the Claflin-Emerson Expedition had camped in 1931, excavated seven small structures and documented 178 archaeological and historic sites, most of them in the previously uninvestigated 11-mile portion of the canyon between the Pace Ranch and the mouth of Nine Mile Canyon. These investigations also resulted in the first significant catalog of radiocarbon dates from the canyon, as well as the first scientific excavations here since John Gillin some 50 years before.

The BYU excavations focused on two residential sites located on a stream terrace above the valley floor—a different topographic setting from those investigated by Gillin (1938) and without a doubt the most common setting for residential sites in Nine Mile Canyon. One of these sites, assigned the moniker "Frank's Place" (42Cb770), featured three possible residential structures that

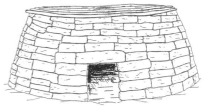

may have been used as temporary dwellings because they had small firepits but almost no midden material. Excavation of the outside use area adjacent…revealed considerable midden material along with numerous firepits and at least one ramada-like structure made of willow and cane. It was in this area that most of the pottery fragments, stone flakes, projectile points and charred food remains were found [Matheny and Alhand 1991:2].

Described as pithouses, the structures were semi-subterranean with wall construction of dry-laid stone masonry. The floor of the larger pithouse was located about 0.5 meters below ground level. The structure had a north-facing entry with a prominent lintel stone. An identical feature was noted at another pithouse located just downslope. The third, smaller pithouse had no discernible entryway (Thompson 1993; Matheny and Alhand 1991:2). The structures at one time probably had wooden beams spanning the distance from wall to wall.

A burial was found in a deep, slab-lined cist located below the floor of the largest of the three pithouses. An analysis of the bone indicated that the individual was an adolescent who suffered from metabolic stress, a chronic advanced tooth infection initiated by trauma to the mouth, and a debilitating congenital back condition. The teeth exhibited considerable wear, a pattern "consistent with the gritty diet of early agriculturalists who processed plants (mostly corn) with stone tools" (Miller 1993:10–11). A Nawthis side-notched projectile point was recovered from the right upper chest region. However, no evidence of traumatic injury was found in the ribs or upper arm bones (1993:13).

A radiocarbon analysis of the burial floor yielded a date of 880 ± 70 BP (cal AD 1018–1281). Charcoal from the floor area of the dwelling returned a radiocarbon date of 1160 ± 70 BP (cal AD 665–1025), a date somewhat earlier than dates of 980 ± 50 BP (cal AD 981–1186) and 980 ± 60 BP (cal AD 904–1210) from an associated hearth and exterior work area (Thompson 1993:103).

The Brigham Young University field school excavated two additional sites. Site 42Dc619 was a pithouse structure similar to Frank's Place, and 42Dc618 was a nearby work area that was probably associated with the pithouse. Both sites were located about 1 mile downstream (east) from Frank's Place. The pithouse exhibited the same characteristics of dry-laid masonry construction as noted at Frank's Place except that the entryway faced east. The work area contained abundant midden material, including charcoal, unworked chert, ceramics, numerous slab-stone metates, manos, turtle-back scrapers, flake scrapers, and waste flakes. Among the 20 projectile points recovered, 7 were identified as Rose Spring corner-notched points and 6 as Uinta side-notched points, and 7 had no identifying diagnostic features (Matheny and Alhand 1991:3). Charcoal from a pithouse hearth yielded a radiocarbon date of 880 ± 50 BP (cal AD 1173), a date statistically identical to those from nearby Frank's Place. Collectively, these dates (Thompson 1993:103) corresponded to the narrow temporal range suggested by tree-ring dates from Sky House (Ferguson 1949; Schulman 1948, 1951).

The BYU Surveys

The Brigham Young University surveys of lower Nine Mile Canyon were initially confined to the area around the historic Pace Ranch, at the time owned by Richard Calder. The Claflin-Emerson Expedition had superficially surveyed this area in 1931 (Gunnerson 1969; Scott 1931a), and Gunnerson (1957) later visited the same area but described only Nordell's Fort (42Dc5). The BYU surveys eventually expanded to include the entire

Typical residential structure in lower Nine Mile Canyon. Photo by Jerry D. Spangler.

canyon area to its confluence with the Green River—spatially the largest single survey ever attempted in Nine Mile Canyon.

Over three field seasons, 151 prehistoric sites were documented, primarily dwellings, storage facilities, rock art panels, cairns, rock alignments, and masonry walls of undetermined utility. Most of the prehistoric architectural sites that were recorded exhibited characteristics of sedentism and/or horticulture commonly attributed to a broader Fremont lifeway, although surveyors noted the rarity of diagnostic artifacts throughout the survey area. That some prehistoric residents of Nine Mile Canyon were at least semi-sedentary was implied by the abundance of stone masonry architecture. Much of the architecture exhibited elaborate and energy-expensive construction. Horticulture was certainly part of the local subsistence strategy, as maize was observed at 11 sites. Ceramics do not appear to have been a significant part of the local lifeway. Of the 151 prehistoric sites recorded, only 25 contained potsherds, none in significant quantities (Spangler 1993).

The distribution of sites is similar to that noted in other areas of Nine Mile Canyon. Residential sites tended to be located on stream terraces 50 to 125 feet above the floodplain, and most were either surface or semi-subterranean structures with horizontally laid slabs defining the walls. They were typically 7 to 16 feet in diameter. The survey recorded 27 residential sites and 43 residential structures. Eighteen of the sites contained

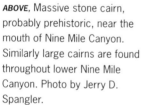

ABOVE, Massive stone cairn, probably prehistoric, near the mouth of Nine Mile Canyon. Similarly large cairns are found throughout lower Nine Mile Canyon. Photo by Jerry D. Spangler.

UPPER RIGHT, Desolation Village, a defensible cluster of surface residences along a narrow butte with a single access point. Photo by Jerry D. Spangler.

LOWER RIGHT, Small circular structure, dubbed a "playpen" by the BYU field school. These are common in lower Nine Mile, but their purpose is unknown. Photo by Jerry D. Spangler.

a single semi-subterranean or surface structure, five contained two such structures, and two had three dwelling structures. Two sites were potential villages, one with eight residential structures and the other with nine. The residential sites were located on stream terraces on both the south and north sides of the canyon, although residential sites were more frequently located on the south side (Spangler 1993).

There was also an abundance of impressive architectural features located on pinnacles, buttes, and rock outcrops, sometimes hundreds of feet above the valley floor and in easily defensible positions. The structures were all constructed on bedrock and featured dry-laid stone masonry. Some were elaborately constructed, while others were little more than circles of stone one to three courses high. Artifacts of any kind were rare at these sites (Spangler 1993). Also unique to lower Nine Mile Canyon were massive stone cairns and tiny circular structures—far too small for residences and unlike anything known for storage—perched on the edges of cliffs (Spangler 1993).

Storage structures of a variety of shapes and sizes were recorded. At least 20 sites were labeled as exclusively storage sites, while an additional nine dwelling sites had associated storage structures, usually subterranean cists located inside or adjacent to the residences. Storage structures were of several types: (1) small slab-lined cists made up of four to seven vertical stones and usually associated with dwelling structures; (2) structures of

The "Shroom Room," an isolated pinnacle tower identified and documented by the BYU field school in 1991. Photo by Jerry D. Spangler.

UPPER, Ray Matheny, of the BYU field school, removes the capstone from an intact granary, one of a series of small chambers situated high on a cliff face and accessible only with a long ladder. Photo by Jerry D. Spangler.

BYU 9 MILE
25 MAY 91
SITE 62

LOWER, This small, easily accessible "granary" structure, documented by the 1991 field school, is typical of lower Nine Mile Canyon. Photo by Jerry D. Spangler.

stone slabs and adobe construction situated on narrow cliff ledges where access is extremely difficult; (3) square or rectangular block-like structures of stones and adobe, also situated on cliff ledges; (4) camouflaged structures of pole, stone, and adobe located in small rockshelters; and (5) adobe and stone structures of various shapes with large, adobe, collar-like entrances, also located in small rockshelters but with no evidence of attempts at concealment (Spangler 1993).

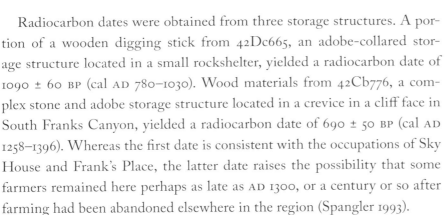

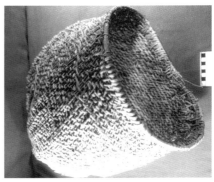

Radiocarbon dates were obtained from three storage structures. A portion of a wooden digging stick from 42Dc665, an adobe-collared storage structure located in a small rockshelter, yielded a radiocarbon date of 1090 ± 60 BP (cal AD 780–1030). Wood materials from 42Cb776, a complex stone and adobe storage structure located in a crevice in a cliff face in South Franks Canyon, yielded a radiocarbon date of 690 ± 50 BP (cal AD 1258–1396). Whereas the first date is consistent with the occupations of Sky House and Frank's Place, the latter date raises the possibility that some farmers remained here perhaps as late as AD 1300, or a century or so after farming had been abandoned elsewhere in the region (Spangler 1993).

Also noteworthy, crews recovered a remarkably well preserved basket that exhibited a weaving technique more akin to that of later Ancestral Ute peoples. The willow basket yielded a radiocarbon date of 395 ± 70 BP (cal AD 1410–1650), and shredded juniper bark from a nearby cist (42Cb779) yielded a date of 250 ± 60 BP (cal AD 1484–1948) (Matheny et al. 1991:4), providing evidence that the prehistoric occupation of Nine Mile Canyon persisted long after the Fremont farmers had given up on agriculture. These hunters and gatherers—probably ancestors of the modern Utes—were present in the canyon at about AD 1500.

Settlement patterns in lower Nine Mile Canyon are consistent with Fremont manifestations observed elsewhere on the northern Colorado

Panoramic view of lower Nine Mile Canyon. This area is now roadless. Photo by Jerry D. Spangler.

Plateau. Residential sites generally consisted of one to three semi-subterranean pithouses located on terraces offering immediate access to permanent water and arable lands. Village sites were rare and were generally small, featuring fewer than a dozen residences. Sunstone Village (42Dc699) and Desolation Village (42Un1926) were both located on narrow mesas with precipitous drops on all but a single narrow access point, suggesting a defensive orientation. The residential architecture exhibited few internal features, and temporally diagnostic artifacts were rare. The Fremont certainly used pottery, but there is very little evidence that they made it here. Given the small number of potsherds found at any particular site, this technology was but a minor part of their lifeway (Spangler 1993).

The BYU investigations, coupled with the USAS surveys in middle Nine Mile Canyon, were without a doubt the most comprehensive conducted in Nine Mile Canyon up to that time. In many respects, these studies built on the framework established by John Gillin, offering a spatially encompassing view of Nine Mile Canyon settlement patterns through time. At their core, the BYU studies reinforced what Gillin first observed in 1936: some Fremont sites are located in close proximity to the valley floor with efficient access to fields and water, and others are located high on easily defensible ridges and pinnacles. In most cases, sites are small, artifacts are frustratingly rare, and rock art is inexplicably pervasive.

These broad-scaled surveys established a framework for the more comprehensive investigations that would be initiated a decade later. The discovery of massive deposits of natural gas on the plateaus high above the Nine Mile Canyon corridor would, in the early 2000s, result in systematic inventories of ever larger blocks of the canyon ecosystem, from high-elevation plateaus to the canyon corridor itself and the myriad side canyons in between. Unlike the academic interest of the past, these investigations would be driven in large part by compliance with the federal National Historic Preservation Act and by private attempts to reach a delicate balance between the preservation of Nine Mile Canyon's remarkable heritage and the development of the extensive natural gas reserves.

7

Current Perspectives on the Prehistory of Nine Mile Canyon

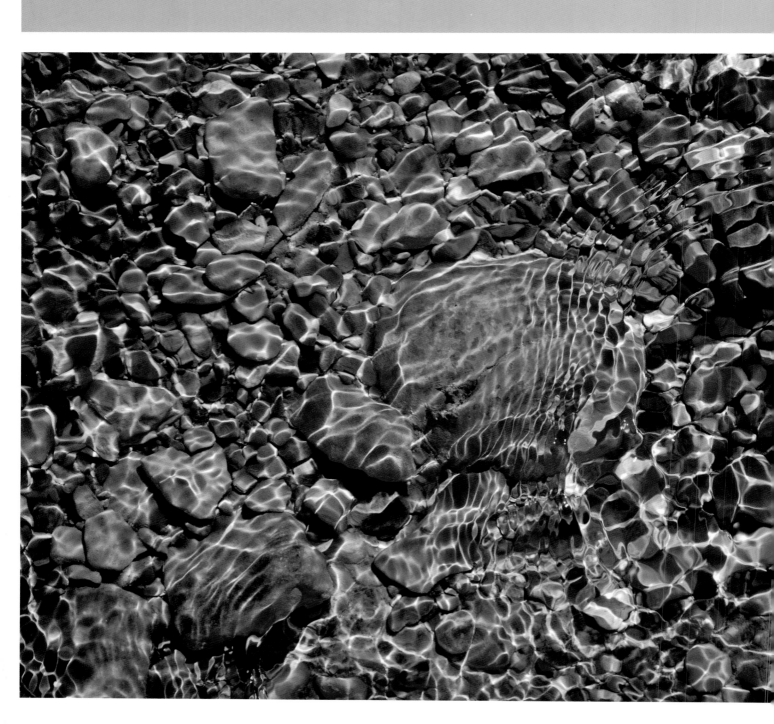

As I re-examine some of my own cross-cultural formulations, I note a long history of changing my mind.... There are perhaps others who...should also change their minds from time-to-time. —JULIAN STEWARD, IN KERNS 2003:109

New Ideas and New Approaches

In the classic fable "The Blind Men and the Elephant," each of the blind men—sometimes it is six, sometimes more—grasps a different part of the elephant. One takes hold of the tail and insists the elephant is a rope; another grabs a leg and says the beast is a tree trunk. Yet another who touches the elephant's ear describes the beast as a winnowing tray, and another who had felt the tusk thought it was a plowshare. And on and on the bickering went, each man insisting he was correct and the others were wrong. As the Buddha (Udana 68–69) mused:

> O how they cling and wrangle, some who claim
> For preacher and monk the honored name!
> For, quarreling, each to his view they cling.
> Such folk see only one side of a thing.

Any archaeologist who has spent time in Nine Mile Canyon has come to recognize that the canyon is indeed like a very large elephant about which we still know very little. The prehistory of Nine Mile Canyon has primarily been defined by excavations at Valley Village and Sky House (Gillin 1938), at Rasmussen Cave (Gunnerson 1969), and at Frank's Place (Thompson 1993)—each of them offering a mere glimpse of one part of a much bigger whole. In fact, we may not yet understand the entire elephant at all.

Archaeological research in Nine Mile Canyon is now undergoing a wide-ranging renaissance. Tens of thousands of hours are expended every year documenting the canyon's seemingly inexhaustible cultural resources. And still, the answers to the canyon's perplexing secrets remain frustratingly

OPPOSITE, Water was the lifeblood of Nine Mile Canyon and the farmers who lived there. Photo by Ray Boren.

Typical surface masonry in Nine Mile Canyon. Photo by Jerry D. Spangler.

elusive—enough so that those working in the canyon are reluctant to offer for public consumption anything but general observations, always couched with words like "could," "might," and "perhaps." Quite simply, serious archaeological inquiry here, even with all the modern scientific tools at our disposal, is still in its infancy, and the unknowns simply outweigh what we do know about the canyon.

That could—there's that word "could" again—change over the next decade. The Bill Barrett Corporation of Denver, Colorado, is harvesting rich reserves of natural gas from its wells high on the Tavaputs Plateau above Nine Mile Canyon. As part of the company's compliance with federal regulations, vast areas of the plateau have already been investigated for their archaeological resources, and more of the region, including portions of Nine Mile Canyon itself, will be studied in the years ahead. The company has also pledged a $3 million archaeological research fund to foster serious scholarly inquiry in the canyon—the largest voluntary contribution for archaeological research in the state's history. This research will undoubtedly change—perhaps radically so—our understanding of the prehistory of Nine Mile Canyon.

Fremont Perspectives

In 1993, I first proposed the term "Tavaputs adaptation" to describe a Fremont presence in the Nine Mile Canyon region that was quite different from the one to the north in the Uinta Basin or to the southwest in the San Rafael Swell (Spangler 1993, 2000a, 2000b). Back then, the sample of radiocarbon and tree-ring dates was small but suggested that the Tavaputs adaptation reached its zenith between about AD 1000 and 1150, and could have lingered as late as AD 1300 in isolated areas.

The "Tavaputs adaptation" is predicated on certain basic assumptions:

- The sheer number of storage localities and suspected residential features—in Nine Mile, Range Creek, and Desolation Canyons they number in the hundreds—and the narrow range of radiocarbon and tree-ring dates for the region collectively point to a rapid and unprecedented population increase, beginning about AD 950, reaching a peak about 1050, and then declining to a point where the human presence becomes almost imperceptible after 1150.

- Although different storage strategies were employed, the presence of large granaries on inaccessible cliff faces and camouflaged cists hidden away in rockshelters suggests that stored food was left unattended for periods of time and that families were not always present to protect their food from "thieves."

- The rarity of ceramics and household trash at residential sites are indicative of high mobility. Pottery is heavy and bulky, and it is ill-suited to families always on the move. And people were simply not staying in any one location long enough for large quantities of trash to accumulate there.

The idea that the Fremont expression found in Nine Mile Canyon was "different" from that of their contemporaries elsewhere was hardly a unique idea. Noel Morss had hinted at differences in his classic monograph of the Fremont culture, as had Julian Steward, Albert Reagan, and John Gillin, the last of whom lamented that Nine Mile Canyon "house types, pottery and stone work fail to fall into the classical complexes" (1938:21). And it was hardly news that the Tavaputs efflorescence occurred at a time when radical changes were under way elsewhere in the Greater Southwest—the so-called Pueblo II expansion, when farming populations expanded to high

Pecked images are ubiquitous in Nine Mile Canyon, but the ancients also painted with red, white, black, yellow, orange, and even blue pigments. Photo by Jerry D. Spangler.

plateaus and previously unexploited canyon drainages. Researchers such as Richard Ambler (1969) and James Gunnerson (1960) had once used the Nine Mile Canyon tree-ring dates, among other evidence, to argue that the entire Fremont culture could be attributed to events occurring during this narrow period of time, an idea now rejected because of decades of research showing that the Fremont were present throughout Utah centuries before.

However, the period from AD 900 to 1300 was indeed a time of considerable sociopolitical stress throughout the Colorado Plateau. The first half of this period was characterized by favorable climates and population expansion. The latter half is typically described in the context of periodic and persistent droughts (Benson et al. 2007) and a concurrent increase in social and political stress (LeBlanc 1999; Turner and Turner 1999). This resulted in competition that prompted defensive responses across the Southwest, including the Tavaputs Plateau. The rarity of radiocarbon or tree-ring dates before about AD 950 and a comparative abundance of dates after that time suggest a rather sudden appearance of Fremont farmers in the region, perhaps due to migration from the San Rafael region to the southwest. It is also possible that the sudden occupations in Nine Mile represent an expansion or migration of Fremont peoples from the Uinta Basin to the north, although Uinta Basin traits (e.g., jacal residential structures

Long-legged shorebirds are especially common in one particular area of Nine Mile Canyon, near Currant Canyon. Photo courtesy of the Colorado Plateau Archaeological Alliance, Ogden, Utah.

with adobe features, Classic Vernal style rock art, limestone-tempered pottery) are not common in the West Tavaputs Plateau.

Madsen and Simms (1998) and Geib (1996) have effectively argued for an apparent breakdown in the Colorado River ethnic boundary at about AD 1000, when the occupations north of the Colorado River become indistinguishable from those to the south—in effect, a mixing of Fremont and Ancestral Puebloan traits. Talbot (2000:182) maintains that the breakdown occurred at about AD 900, as evidenced by the appearance of new architectural styles and forms indicative of Ancestral Puebloan expansionism and interface with Fremont populations. In the Tavaputs Plateau, especially in Nine Mile Canyon, these changes were associated with what appears to be a defensive posture, suggesting a level of competition not evident before that time. Given the complexity and radical nature of this defensive shift, it likely involved the movement of substantial numbers of people, as well as ideas and trade goods.

Making Sense of Pots

Madsen and Simms (1998) have suggested that the Tavaputs adaptation may be nothing more than a shift of San Rafael Fremont peoples into the Tavaputs Plateau when conditions warranted, and that farmsteads in the

Each petroglyph involves thousands of individual "dints" to remove patina, or the natural rust weathering, from the cliff face. Not only was it time-consuming, but it required exceptional skill. Photo courtesy of the Colorado Plateau Archaeological Alliance, Ogden, Utah.

Tavaputs Plateau were logistically connected to farming communities a considerable distance to the southwest. If the Tavaputs adaptation represents a population shift from the San Rafael Swell to a new residence, it would be expected that Tavaputs ceramics would be made from local materials, as is the case throughout Utah. But

> in fact, the dominance of exotic ceramics [apparently basalt temper] suggests a logistical connection to the San Rafael Swell area, a pattern where vessels manufactured to the south were brought in relatively small quantity to the Tavaputs sites when the defensive regime was operating. This is consistent with the relative infrequency of ceramics, little evidence for local manufacture, the slightly higher presence of Anasazi [Ancestral Puebloan] trade wares, and the rarity of ceramics at Tavaputs Plateau forager sites [Madsen and Simms 1998:309].

The rarity of ceramics in Nine Mile Canyon and elsewhere in the Tavaputs Plateau has perplexed archaeologists for decades. In a 1932 exchange of letters between Noel Morss, the father of the Fremont culture concept, and John Otis Brew, the renowned southwestern archaeologist at the Peabody Museum, Morss lamented that "we found pottery so scarce in certain sites in the Fremont district as to suggest that perhaps there was a

Grayware pottery from Nine Mile Canyon. This example has dark stone tempering, perhaps basalt. Photo courtesy of the Colorado Plateau Archaeological Alliance, Ogden, Utah.

time when, if not entirely absent, it was perhaps not made locally" (Morss 1932). Decades later, I referred to this phenomenon as the "one-pot pit-house" (Spangler 2000a) to describe the fact that none of the suspected pithouses in Nine Mile Canyon had more than a few scattered potsherds; many had none whatsoever.

Although the surface evidence is scant, most of the potsherds observed during broad-scale surveys over the past two decades appear to have been tempered with dark crushed rock that has the appearance of the basalt-tempered grayware so common in the San Rafael Swell. Basalt is not found anywhere in the Tavaputs Plateau, however. This, of course, has led to assumptions about a logistical connection toward the southwest in the San Rafael Swell, rather than the Uinta Basin, where Fremont people preferred limestone or calcite tempering. But the reality may be much more complicated than that. Recent excavations at two sites in Nine Mile Canyon revealed that most of grayware potsherds there were more akin to those of the Uinta Basin, not the San Rafael Swell (Patterson 2009; Jody Patterson, personal communication 2011). However, limestone is also extremely rare in the Tavaputs Plateau.

The resolution of this question has important implications for our understanding of the prehistory of Nine Mile Canyon. The shape, size, and

construction techniques of ceramics can all offer important insights into where the ancient Fremont came from and whether or not these groups were sedentary or mobile. They can also provide clues about technological changes in prehistoric societies. Elsewhere in the Southwest, researchers have argued that ceramics marked a fundamental shift at about AD 600 toward cultivation of protein-rich beans—a food resource that requires two to three hours of boiling to become digestible (Reed et al. 2000).

The Fremont of Nine Mile Canyon clearly knew about ceramics, but they chose not to use this technology to any great extent. Why? There is minimal evidence (yet) that they ever manufactured pottery here, preferring instead to transport it into the canyon in small quantities. Why? Based on the presence of distinctive Ancestral Puebloan black-on-white and polychrome potsherds at a handful of sites, we know that they at least had some trade connections to groups hundreds of miles to the south (or at the very least to other Fremont groups that had those connections). More puzzling is why they chose not to make their jugs, ollas, and bowls at their Nine Mile Canyon homes—a much more energy-efficient and cost-effective strategy even if the vessels are produced only in small quantities.

Theories about long-distance transport of ceramics into the Tavaputs Plateau are predicated on long-held assumptions that the predominant graywares in the region were tempered with basalt or limestone from

The Family Panel. Photo by Jerry D. Spangler.

regions far distant. However, what if the tempering agent of the local Nine Mile grayware was not basalt, but rather some other crushed stone that is available locally but has the outward appearance of basalt? And what if limestone is more abundant here than we realize? As yet, the mineral content of the graywares found at sites in the Tavaputs Plateau has not been examined by scientists. Future research could well determine that the grayware utilitarian vessels used in Nine Mile Canyon and elsewhere in the region were indeed manufactured locally and with locally available materials, but never in significant quantities.

Drought and Decline

The suspected social conflict hypothesized for the later Fremont period in the Tavaputs Plateau and elsewhere on the northern Colorado Plateau clearly occurred in the context of major and persistent droughts that plagued much of the western United States. In particular, three droughts— one in the late AD 900s to early 1000s, another in the mid AD 1100s, and yet another in the late AD 1200s—appear to have had far-reaching impacts. As argued by Benson et al. (2007), the first drought coincided with dramatic population declines (or population shifts to new localities) among the Fremont living in northeastern Utah and the eastern Great Basin, indicated by a marked decline in the radiocarbon frequency curves after AD 1000 (Berry and Berry 2003) and the appearance of defensive strategies in the Tavaputs Plateau (Spangler 2002). The second drought resulted in the abandonment of most of the great houses in the central San Juan Basin and in population declines throughout the Southwest, including the Tavaputs Plateau. The third drought resulted in the abandonment of remaining population centers, including the last remnants in the Tavaputs Plateau, beginning about AD 1280.

The effect of these droughts on Fremont populations is poorly understood, and population expansion and contraction was not synchronous across the entire Fremont region. Based on radiocarbon frequency curves, population declines may have occurred in the northeastern Great Basin at AD 1050, 1160, and 1290 (Berry and Berry 2003), and in the Uinta Basin by about AD 1000 (Spangler 2002). In the greater Uinta Basin, which includes the Tavaputs Plateau, there may have been an overall population decline that began during the drought of the mid AD 1100s, the same time when defensive responses were evident. The latest radiocarbon dates here occur during the middle to late AD 1200s and are very few in number (Benson et al. 2007; Spangler 2002).

Recent research by the Tree-Ring Laboratory at the University of Arizona has contributed new insights into Nine Mile Canyon drought sequences (Knight et al. 2009). Tree-ring records point to a horrific drought in the early AD 500s—a drought so severe it was beyond anything known in modern times. Prolonged dry conditions also occurred before AD 830 and again in the mid to late AD 900s, while wetter conditions were evident in the AD 1000s—when the Tavaputs adaptation would have been at its apex. Extended dry spells returned to the region by the AD 1100s and continued through 1300—a two-century-long period when there is decreasing evidence of agriculture in the Tavaputs Plateau. In general, what researchers found was that local climates were extremely unpredictable from year to year and decade to decade, and that unusually dry episodes lasting 20 to 30 years or more could have had devastating effects on farmers who had become accustomed to earlier, atypically wet conditions.

The tree-ring data are intriguing in that they present a finer-scale perspective of local prehistoric climates as wildly unpredictable and perhaps unsuitable to agriculture for extended periods of time. But we should be

"Currant Village." Photo courtesy of the Colorado Plateau Archaeological Alliance, Ogden, Utah.

cautious about inferring that droughts caused an abandonment of farming in Nine Mile Canyon. Evidence suggests that Fremont farmers used irrigation ditches to water their crops, much as modern farmers do today. And, historically, Nine Mile Creek and Range Creek flow even in the worst droughts. They may not carry as much water, but they carry water nonetheless, likely enough to support at least some of the Fremont population.

Research elsewhere in the Southwest suggests that it is not the amount of rainfall that influences the viability of farming but the nature of the rainfall. Droughts can produce low water tables, and when the summer monsoons arrive, the stream channels are much more vulnerable to severe erosion, called arroyo-cutting or down-cutting (Dernbach 1992). In effect, the water is still there, but it becomes increasingly difficult to divert out of the ever-deepening stream channels that result from violent summer thunderstorms. In the Grand Staircase region, this pattern of down-cutting occurred after a prolonged wet cycle that coincided with explosive population growth. Population declines there coincided with increased down-cutting.

It is not known whether down-cutting contributed to the collapse of the Tavaputs adaptation (the geomorphology studies simply haven't been conducted). But the pattern is strikingly similar: a period of explosive population growth during favorable climates, followed by a rapid population decline during deteriorating climates.

The Bigfoot Panel. Photo by Jerry D. Spangler.

Looking to the Sierra Tarahumara

One of the more perplexing problems facing archaeologists working in Nine Mile Canyon is the sheer number of archaeological sites but the otherwise minimal evidence that anyone lived there for any length of time. But what if there were only a few families living in Nine Mile Canyon, each of which constructed a large number of separate residences and storage structures at optimal field locations as they moved up and down the canyon? K. Renee Barlow, the former curator at the Prehistoric Museum at the College of Eastern Utah in Price, raised that possibility in her model for Fremont agriculture, looking to northern Mexico for an example (2002, 2006).

In the Sierra Tarahumara, maize farmers occupy multiple residences associated with different maize fields. Each family dries and stores crops in numerous small, detached stone storage "cribs." Isolated cribs and granaries are made of wood, stone, or stone plus adobe, and are located near habitation structures, are incorporated into the walls of distant rockshelters or caves, or are solitary structures near remote maize fields. In the 1700s, Tarahumara farmers also built small stone structures on cliff faces high above streams. The Tarahumara typically cultivate one to four fields, occasionally as many as six. It is not uncommon for families to move frequently between different fields, which may be up to 6 or 7 miles apart. Smaller, more remote fields were used as contingencies against the failure of crops elsewhere. Surplus food is commonly stored near the fields where it was produced and is retrieved as needed. Habitations include various types of constructed houses and south-facing rockshelters (Barlow 2002; Pennington 1963).

RIGHT, Nine Mile Canyon granary.
Photo by Ray Boren.

LEFT, Small, easily accessible
granary in Nine Mile Canyon.
No attempt was made to
conceal it from passersby.
Photo courtesy of the Colorado
Plateau Archaeological Alliance,
Ogden, Utah.

If the Tarahumara strategy, or some variation of it, was being practiced by the Fremont in Nine Mile Canyon, the number of residences and nearby storage structures would be far greater than the number of people who lived there at one time. Instead of dozens or scores of families, the roughly 40 miles of cultivable Nine Mile floodplain could have been divided among just a few families, each with a series of small field houses and nearby storage structures. Because of the frequent moves between their different field houses, few artifacts would have been left behind at any one site.

Jody Patterson, the lead archaeologist on projects related to the Bill Barrett Corporation's West Tavaputs Plateau natural gas project, recently suggested that possibility. He examined a small portion of Nine Mile Canyon, looking at the spatial distribution of granaries and residential sites, the volume of the granaries, the potential yields per acre, and the amount of corn needed to support an individual in a given year. In the small area between Water Canyon and Cottonwood Canyon, he identified 33 granaries, ranging from 10 to 150 feet above the ground, most of them accessible without the need of ladders or ropes. Granaries on inaccessible cliff faces were rare (Patterson and Flanigan 2010).

In general, Patterson's research lends support to the idea that small groups of farmers were moving between different fields and storing their crops in adjacent granaries for later retrieval.

ABOVE, A large granary with smaller associated granaries, all located on an inaccessible cliff face in Range Creek Canyon. Photo courtesy of the Colorado Plateau Archaeological Alliance, Ogden, Utah.

RIGHT, Inaccessible cliff granary in Range Creek Canyon. Note how cantilevers were used to support its outer edge. Photo courtesy of the Colorado Plateau Archaeological Alliance, Ogden, Utah.

A small population of people could likely support themselves and store enough grain for future uncertainties with little problem. The balance between population and resources, however, was probably tenuous. The association of grain storage facilities, probable field locations, and habitations suggests to us that the inhabitants likely continually farmed the same areas regularly [Patterson and Flanigan 2010:7].

Barlow's research in nearby Range Creek has identified a similar strategy there, but she raises the possibility that Fremont storage strategies changed through time. In Range Creek, there are a many small granaries in close proximity to houses and fields, as in Nine Mile Canyon. But there are also a large number of very inaccessible granaries high on cliff faces—far more than are evident in Nine Mile Canyon. The largest are located on cliff faces high above pithouse villages and maize fields. Others are located a substantial distance from permanent water and potential fields, and some are not visible from the nearest known residence (Barlow et al. 2008).

Applying a model based on animal behavior (see Vander Wall 1990), Barlow believes that storage of food in large granaries, called larder hoarding, is evidence of a relatively large, sedentary population that will vigorously defend the stored food. In contrast, storage of food in many scattered, small granaries near fields, called scatter hoarding, is evidence of high mobility. Simply put, scatter hoards are evidence that those who produced the food were not always there to protect their stored food, and there was probably some expectation that some but not all the food would be lost to rodents or thieves.

Evidence from Range Creek, which may be comparable to Nine Mile Canyon, suggests that the Fremont farmers there were highly successful farmers who used a variety of storage tactics at different points in time. From about AD 400 to 860, the canyon was used by small household groups of highly mobile foragers who farmed different locations and stored food in dispersed caches. They would later return to consume or retrieve their food. Farming may have been important, but it likely consisted mainly of planting and harvesting, and there was probably minimal investment in replanting, weeding, and watering fields during the growing season (Barlow et al. 2008; see also Barlow 2002).

Barlow believes that between AD 950 and 1050, people in nearby Fremont and Puebloan regions were intensifying farming, becoming more sedentary, and likely experiencing population increases and greater nutritional stress. In Range Creek, people mainly occupied small seasonal settlements of one to three pithouses, stored their food in hidden caches and in large remote granaries on cliffs, and also continued hunting and collecting wild seeds (Barlow et al. 2008).

Barlow has also argued that the Fremont in Range Creek retained a fairly high degree of residential mobility relative to Fremont in other regions at that time, all within the context of increasing population and greater competition for resources that resulted in the evolution of a unique storage strategy, mainly in cliff granaries at locations some distance from residences. She believes that this was likely a form of resource defense and that the Fremont families of Range Creek were fearful of raids during this time. By AD 1060, there was an increase in sedentism and a shift away from the use of cliff granaries.

A marked decrease in the use of remote cliff granaries in the 1100s indicates that this strategy was no longer used. The larger Range Creek settlements are likely indicative of moderate population aggregation and possibly an increase in sedentism associated with increases in the intensity of agricultural practices. Rather than increased

stability, however, the intensive use of one or few agricultural fields may have increased the risk of agricultural shortfall, while simultaneously decreasing access to previously used wild food collection areas. Ultimately, a shift to greater sedentism may not have been the most successful adaptation in the Range Creek drainage [Barlow et al. 2008:41–42].

By the AD 1100s, the Fremont farmers in Range Creek may have occupied only a handful of farming villages in the middle and lower portions of the canyon. These sites include multiple pithouses with middens, where there is evidence of an increase in sedentism, residential storage, and more aggressive defense of stored food. In this period, Range Creek farming villages may have been occupied only during some years, and there were fewer but larger settlements (Barlow et al. 2008). The construction of masonry habitation and storage facilities appears to have ceased in Range Creek by about AD 1200.

Keeping a Watchful Eye

One component of the Tavaputs adaptation that could use revision is the idea that the very large granaries high on inaccessible cliff faces are evidence of periodic abandonment. Shannon Arnold-Boomgarden at the

University of Utah has examined the distribution of large granaries in Range Creek, and she has proposed that such granaries are, in fact, evidence of a resident population that will vigorously defend the stored food. Using digital elevation models (DEMs) and high-resolution aerial photographs, she examined the viewsheds for 54 granaries, all of which are visible from the valley floor or from another site location, although sometimes they are hard to see because of distance or the use of local construction materials that make them blend into the cliff face. Her preliminary study demonstrates that Fremont granaries in the main canyon were not purposely hidden from view, but rather were situated to allow their owners "to easily identify potential thieves approaching or attempting to access stored food." Furthermore, "the topography of this region is so rugged and varied that we suspect the Fremont could have just as easily concealed them completely," but they intentionally chose not to do so (Arnold-Boomgarden 2008:1; see also 2009).

In Range Creek Canyon, granaries high on the cliff faces appear to share a combination of the scatter hoarding and larder hoarding characteristics defined by Vander Wall (1990). Scatter hoards are typically hidden and left unattended, are usually numerous, and contain only small amounts of a resource so that if one is pilfered or the contents otherwise lost the hoarder does not lose everything. Larder hoards are usually fewer in number, are larger, and are situated closer to a residence, making the stored foods easy to retrieve and defend. Arnold-Boomgarden concludes:

> Thus, in Range Creek Canyon, it appears that the small cists and granaries hidden in easily accessible locations (i.e. boulder fields and alcoves) are much like the scatter hoarding strategy. On the other hand, the "remote" granaries are more like larder hoards in size but they are scattered across the landscape in difficult-to-access but highly visible and easy-to-monitor locations. So while they are not actively guarded, they are protected from pilferage by their difficulty to access and high visibility. In this situation the cost of guarding is reduced. Placing a granary on public display increases the number of witnesses and spreads the cost of guarding among all participants. This increases the benefits of locating granaries in such seemingly costly locations [Arnold-Boomgarden 2009:18].

One of several large and inaccessible cliff granaries in middle Nine Mile Canyon. Photo courtesy of the Colorado Plateau Archaeological Alliance, Ogden, Utah.

How might these studies relate to Nine Mile Canyon? Nine Mile Canyon has the same types of granaries as Range Creek. The prevalence of small, easily accessible granaries, all in close proximity to potential fields and residences, is indeed consistent with models proposed by Patterson and Barlow of family groups moving between different fields and caching their produce for later retrieval. The comparative scarcity of the large, inaccessible granaries in Nine Mile Canyon—there are several in Nine Mile but not in the numbers evident in Range Creek—could be interpreted as evidence that Nine Mile Canyon had a much smaller resident population to aggressively defend a concentration of stored food.

Long-Distance Farming

As archaeologists more and more look to the Tarahumara of northern Mexico and other groups as analogs for Fremont farming strategies, an important question arises: How far afield would the Fremont farmers go to plant, tend, harvest, and store their maize? The Tarahumara model suggests that each family would tend up to four, or occasionally up to six, fields along 6 to 7 miles of the canyon bottom. Those fields farthest away would be "contingency fields"—an insurance plan against failure of crops closer to home. Recent research in Desolation Canyon along the Green River (Spangler and Jones 2009) raises the possibility that Fremont farmers could have been tending fields 10 or 20 or even 30 miles from the main population centers in Nine Mile Canyon and Range Creek. And that barely hints at the distances involved moving up and down the 90-mile-long Green River corridor to tend fields.

In Desolation Canyon, there is an abundance of granaries, large ones and small ones but only a few that could be interpreted as "defensive" in that access to them was very difficult. And residential structures—the semi-subterranean pithouses that characterize settlement patterns in Nine Mile Canyon and Range Creek—are rare. Only eight have so far been documented along more than 90 miles of river corridor. Evidence of temporary occupations of rockshelters, however, is quite abundant.

Collectively, the Desolation Canyon evidence supports the assumptions about temporary, perhaps seasonal occupations by prehistoric farmers who did not remain in the canyon corridor for significant periods of time. This is reflected in the temporary use of rockshelters, some with casual rock alignments or dry-laid stone walls, and in the open dune occupations more characteristic of seasonal encampments, as well as the generally sparse artifacts at all sites. None of these sites had substantial middens, and temporally diagnostic artifacts were rare. Indeed, the scarcity of artifacts of any kind at any site type was remarkable. Roughly half of all sites had no artifacts whatsoever, and almost all others had fewer than 20 artifacts per site (Spangler and Jones 2009).

The peculiarity of Desolation Canyon is the sheer number of granaries but a lack of any convincing evidence of year-round occupation; evidence of winter occupation has yet to be documented here. There are at least 51 storage features at 35 different sites. These features are predominantly granaries (n = 47) that were constructed of vertical and/or horizontal sandstone slabs, adobe, and wooden poles. The structures are generally moderate to large in size. However, two of the largest structures had no remaining adobe or wood in the construction matrix, and these two may not have been granaries (Spangler and Jones 2009).

By comparison, only eight structures of suspected residential use were identified at six different sites in Desolation Canyon, and all had few, if any, artifacts. In fact, the rarity of evidence that any of these farmers invested time or energy in the construction of residences would seem to support the idea that small groups of farmers came into the canyon in the spring to plant their maize, moving frequently up and down the river corridor to tend their crops but never staying in any one place long enough for

Small granary of the type common to Desolation Canyon, easily accessible and only minimally concealed. Former Utah state archaeologist Kevin Jones and Kristen Jensen of the Division of State History investigate this small granary near Flat Canyon. Photo courtesy of the Colorado Plateau Archaeological Alliance, Ogden, Utah.

Inaccessible granaries high on cliff faces are rare in Desolation Canyon, but those found here are all located near a likely residence. Photo courtesy of the Colorado Plateau Archaeological Alliance, Ogden, Utah.

significant household trash to accumulate around them. Instead of formal residences, they likely used small rockshelters as temporary domiciles. In the fall, maize was harvested and stored in nearby granaries for retrieval as needed, and the farming families abandoned the Green River in favor of a winter residence elsewhere (Spangler and Jones 2009).

How does this all relate to what was happening at the same time in Nine Mile Canyon and Range Creek? In many respects, the pattern described by Arnold-Boomgarden—large granaries on inaccessible cliff faces situated to be observed and protected by a resident population—holds true in some areas of Desolation Canyon. Five of the six largest granaries documented in the Green River corridor are located within 650 feet of a likely residential site—close enough that they could be monitored by a sedentary population. The scattering of small-to-medium, readily accessible storage facilities would appear consistent with the models proposed by Patterson and Flanigan (2010) and Arnold-Boomgarden (2008, 2009): seasonal occupation by highly mobile Fremont farmers who moved between multiple fields and cached their food near their fields for later retrieval. When the Tavaputs Plateau data are considered as a whole, it becomes increasingly evident that this pattern is the same from one area to another, but with interesting twists unique to each place.

This style of pecking is called "stipple" pecking, in which just enough of the patina is removed to create the desired image. Photo by Jerry D. Spangler.

An important question persists: Were the temporary farmers of Desolation Canyon in fact highly mobile farmers who returned to spend the winter months in Range Creek and Nine Mile Canyon? If so, what are the implications of annual mobility involving fields 20 or 30 miles distant? Or have we not yet discovered these farmers' winter residences, which may be much closer to Desolation Canyon, perhaps in the still mostly unexplored Green River side canyons like Flat Canyon, Jack Canyon, Trail Canyon, and Rock Creek Canyon? Still, it raises the possibility that Desolation Canyon—all 90 miles of it—was utilized by ancient farmers as "contingency fields" by the residents of Nine Mile Canyon and Range Creek as an expansive insurance policy against crop failure. It also raises the intriguing prospect that the ancients had an entirely different perspective of distance and that archaeologists should look at much broader landscapes to explain the clues left behind.

Seeking Temporal Order

Most of the recent evidence reported from Nine Mile, Range Creek, and Desolation Canyons continues to support the idea that the Tavaputs Plateau experienced an intense expansion of farming between AD 950 and 1150. But there is also new evidence that the region was occupied long before and long after that period (see graph below). Recent work by Montgomery Archaeological Consultants on the high plateau above Nine Mile Canyon has identified several stone points characteristic of Paleoindian peoples who hunted the last vestiges of Ice Age mammals in the region 8,000 years ago or more (Whitfield et al. 2006). And there is abundant evidence of high-elevation camps used repeatedly by Archaic hunters and gatherers over thousands of years (Spangler et al. 2006; Whitfield et al. 2006). Such evidence remains rare inside the Nine Mile, Range Creek, and Desolation Canyon drainages, but it is probably there.

There is also recent evidence that Fremont farmers were present in the canyon centuries before AD 950 and exploited Nine Mile Canyon in much the same way as later residents. Investigations at 42Dc769, a pithouse in the Nutter Ranch area, demonstrated an occupation by maize-growing, pottery-using, bead-manufacturing groups between about AD 570 and 880 (Patterson 2009:72). The site was interpreted as a residential base from which logistical forays were made to collect wild plants, to hunt wild game, and to plant, tend, and harvest maize being grown on the nearby floodplain (2009:85).

Radiocarbon frequency curve for Nine Mile Canyon, Range Creek, and Desolation Canyon suggesting periods of low-intensity occupation before and after the great Fremont florescence at about AD 1050. Image courtesy of the Colorado Plateau Archaeological Alliance, Ogden, Utah.

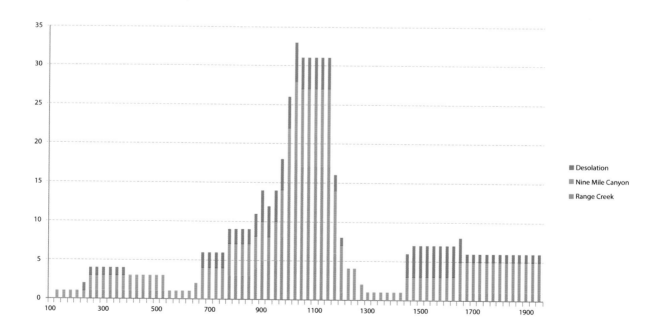

More importantly, this site serves as a reminder that what archaeologists see on the surface may not be indicative of what lies below. When the site was first documented in 1993, only a scattering of surface artifacts was apparent. Later excavations revealed a pithouse and other associated features, none of which was visible on the surface. "That a pithouse and other features with few surface indications were identified at the site hints that many more such sites may exist" (Patterson 2009:85). And it could very well be that the great Fremont florescence from AD 950 to 1150 is an illusion perpetuated by the visibility of those sites on the surface, when in fact earlier occupations lie just below the surface and out of view.

There is also some recent evidence that farming may not have entirely disappeared from this region by AD 1200; rather, small groups of farmers may have remained, exploiting agricultural niches and living alongside hunters and gatherers. This possibility stands in sharp contrast to traditional southwestern models in which a rapid population increase during Pueblo II times was followed by a rapid depopulation and final abandonment between AD 1250 and 1300. But research in nearby Desolation Canyon has called the "abandonment assumption" into question. As discussed in Chapter 6, a radiocarbon date from Nine Mile Canyon, obtained from a corncob, raised the possibility that maize could have been cultivated there as late as AD 1300. But without corroborating evidence, the date was suspect, and certainly not convincing enough to offer definitive statements to that effect.

Recently, two radiocarbon dates were obtained from two different sites near the mouth of Rock Creek, a small tributary to the Green River about 40 miles south of the mouth of Nine Mile Canyon. A corncob recovered from a looted shelter at 42Cb224 returned a radiocarbon date of 240 ± 40 BP (cal AD 1530–1950), and a willow fragment from the construction matrix of a subterranean cist at 42Cb416, which by all appearances was identical to Fremont cists elsewhere, returned a radiocarbon date of 340 ± 40 BP (cal AD 1450–1650). The minimum ranges of both dates are well after archaeologists have assumed agriculture was abandoned in the region. It remains possible that both dates are aberrant—that the samples were somehow contaminated. But the fact that the two dates are from separate features in the same general area reduces that possibility (Spangler and Jones 2009).

Pictographs in Cottonwood Canyon. Photo by Jerry D. Spangler.

That Fremont-like agriculture persisted after AD 1300 is not without precedent in the region generally. Possible Fremont architectural sites in nearby northwestern Colorado have been dated to between AD 1300 and 1600 (Creasman 1981; Creasman and Scott 1987; LaPoint et al. 1981). These bear a striking resemblance to the pinnacle structures described in Nine Mile Canyon. A late Fremont manifestation is also suggested at site 42Un1103 in Dinosaur National Monument (Liestman 1985) and in the Flaming Gorge area at Allen Creek Village, where radiocarbon dates suggest a continuum of Fremont occupation from AD 550 to 1420 (Johnson and Loosle 2002:137). Collectively, these dates suggest that Fremont-like strategies might have persisted in isolated niches in northeastern Utah and northwestern Colorado, and that farming coexisted with the hunting and gathering typically associated with ancestors of the modern Utes. The two radiocarbon dates from Rock Creek raise the intriguing possibility that farming persisted in the Tavaputs Plateau area long after it had been abandoned elsewhere and thus that the late maize date from Nine Mile Canyon should not be rejected out of hand.

Perhaps the most important research development in the Tavaputs Plateau region over the past 20 years has been the establishment of a time frame for certain events. There is evidence that the region was occupied long before and long after AD 1000. Through the combined research efforts under way in Nine Mile, Range Creek, and Desolation Canyons, more than 50 radiocarbon dates have now been reported—a decent sample size that helps minimizes the risk of overly broad interpretations. When the statistical probability of the age ranges of those dates is plotted onto a frequency curve, several interesting possibilities emerge. There is some evidence that farmers arrived in the canyon between AD 250 and 520, but not in significant numbers. There is very little evidence that they were here between AD 520 and 680, which would coincide with a severe drought documented for this region (Knight et al. 2009).

It also appears that Fremont farmers had returned to the Tavaputs Plateau region by about AD 700 and that their numbers increased steadily over the next three centuries. This evidence is found just below the surface at sites that are not always obvious from the surface (see Patterson 2009). The radiocarbon data also lend support to our long-held belief that something dramatic happened here at about AD 1000. In fact, the number of radiocarbon dates with ranges between AD 1000 and 1150 is several times greater than any number before or after that time. The Tavaputs Plateau temporal sequence contrasts sharply with that described for the nearby Uinta Basin, where a relatively continuous occupation of permanent residential sites, all focused on the production of domesticated foods, can be demonstrated from about AD 200 to 1050. A similar temporal sequence is likely in the Tavaputs Plateau, but it is currently underrepresented by radiocarbon dates. Most Tavaputs Plateau residential sites have yielded radiocarbon dates with median intercepts tightly clustered between about AD 1025 and 1175. Recent radiocarbon and tree-ring data from nearby Desolation Canyon and Range Creek offer little to contradict initial conclusions that a Fremont expansion into the Tavaputs Plateau was narrowly confined to the late Fremont period. And then the population seems to have crashed just as abruptly.

Anthropomorphs come in all sizes and shapes in Nine Mile Canyon. This one is rectangular, but others are oval, some are cigar-shaped, and yet others are trapezoidal and circular. Photo by Jerry D. Spangler.

Looking at a Bigger Elephant

As we can see from the foregoing discussion, much of what we "know" about the Fremont of Nine Mile Canyon comes from studies elsewhere— Range Creek, Desolation Canyon, and the high plateaus. But what do archaeologists really know about Nine Mile Canyon? Since 2006, the Colorado Plateau Archaeological Alliance has been working with state and

Large slab-lined cist in upper Nine Mile Canyon, where storage structures are abundant. In one area alone, there are 10 different structures within a half-mile of each other. Photo courtesy of the Colorado Plateau Archaeological Alliance, Ogden, Utah.

federal agencies, industry, and conservation groups to get a better understanding of where sites are located and which sites are vulnerable to looting, trampling by visitors, and industrial development. Seven major surveys have been completed totaling almost 7 square miles of the canyon—to date the largest investigation ever conducted in Nine Mile Canyon. We looked not only at sites along the road familiar to tourists, but at every topographic location from the valley floor to about 1,000 feet above it. We have documented more than 500 sites in every possible topographic setting, from niches and grottoes to pinnacle tops and buttes. The results of our research are tantalizing but preliminary as we build a more statistically valid sample. But certain patterns are evident:

- The number of archaeological sites is indeed staggering. In middle Nine Mile Canyon, between Cottonwood Canyon on the south and Currant Canyon on the north, the density of sites averages between 80 and 120 per square mile—a density that ranks among the highest anywhere in the state of Utah and on a par with the famed Cedar Mesa area of southeastern Utah.

- The density of sites is greatest in settings near the valley floor, and the density decreases proportionally with increased distance above

the valley floor. In short, 70 to 80 percent of all sites are located within the first 330 feet above the valley floor.

- Site density is dramatically less in upper Nine Mile Canyon at elevations where it becomes increasingly risky to grow food. Between about 6,200 and 6,500 feet elevation at the floodplain, the density of sites drops to less than 20 sites per square mile. The types of sites are generally the same as at lower elevations, but there are far fewer of them. There is, however, a greater frequency of storage structures there.

- There is an overwhelming prevalence of rock art sites that exceeds anything reported elsewhere in the state of Utah and maybe even the United States. More than 80 percent of all documented sites have rock art elements, and more than 70 percent are exclusively rock art sites. Indeed, the canyon's moniker of "World's Longest Art Gallery" is well deserved.

- The number of rock art sites tends to overshadow the fact that the ancients were also living here. Prehistoric residences take a wide variety of forms, including stacked masonry one- and two-room

Rock art sites like this one in middle Nine Mile Canyon occur in such numbers that the canyon may be home to the largest concentration of prehistoric images in the United States. Photo courtesy of the Colorado Plateau Archaeological Alliance, Ogden, Utah.

surface structures, semi-subterranean pithouses, D-shaped houses built next to a cliff face, and occasionally casual structures inside rockshelters. With few exceptions, all are small (usually less than 10 feet in diameter) and would have been suitable for a single family. There is no single preferred house style.

- There is no significant difference in the ratio of site types—rock art, storage, and residential—by increased elevation above the valley floor. In total, there may be fewer sites at higher elevations, but the types of sites and their ratio are virtually the same as at lower elevations.

- Evidence of longer-term occupations is indeed rare. Only Warrior Ridge (42Dc1), at three-quarters of a mile long, has significant numbers of artifacts. If Warrior Ridge is excluded from the ample, the number of chipped-stone, groundstone, pottery, and organic artifacts at any given site averages less than one artifact per site.

- Although sites are numerous, they are generally small. Most rock art sites average fewer than 10 images, most granaries occur as a single unit and are less than 10 cubic feet in size, and residences are scattered up and down the canyon with almost no evidence of aggregation into villages (Warrior Ridge is again the exception with four houses in close proximity and at least 10 located along the entire ridge line).

- Patterns are beginning to emerge in the nature and distribution of rock art sites. They are generally clustered in relatively close proximity to suspected residential sites, but not necessarily with storage sites. Certain motifs, such as the horned snake and the dot matrix, are universal, occurring in abundance throughout the canyon. Others, such as the combatants at Warrior Ridge, long-legged shorebirds, and strange linear human figures with upside-down trapezoidal bodies, occur in only small geographic areas of the canyon, usually within a half mile of each other. Classic Fremont anthropomorphs are quite rare.

Summary

As we try to understand the totality of Nine Mile Canyon, we recognize that these observations, based on small areas within the canyon, offer only a glimpse of the whole. Most of the canyon remains uninvestigated and the sites undocumented. We do not know yet if settlement patterns are different from one area of the canyon to another, or whether those patterns changed over time. The elephant in this case is so large that it may be several more decades before the prehistory of Nine Mile Canyon is fully understood.

Archaeologists are still struggling with fundamental questions about how the ancients thrived in this unusually harsh desert environment. Yes, we have a better picture of the "entire elephant," but we do not yet understand how human behavior changed over time, the role of the local environment in those changes, and when those changes might have occurred. The most encouraging thing is that the Tavaputs Plateau has been the focus of serious ongoing scholarly research for nearly a decade, and this research is likely to continue for another two decades as the Bill Barrett Corporation harvests its rich natural gas reserves. Cumulatively, the amount of research being conducted now and into the future will make the Tavaputs Plateau one of the most thoroughly investigated—and potentially one of the best-understood—regions anywhere in the state.

Some might question the prudence of spending millions of dollars to explain a long-vanished people or even the relevance of this research to our society today. Ominously, the dramatic rise and rapid collapse of the Fremont of Nine Mile Canyon and Range Creek and elsewhere on the Tavaputs Plateau is a pattern that could be poised to repeat itself. Archaeologists maintain that prehistoric societies were never more vulnerable to climate-related crises than after a period of exponential population growth resulting from a favorable climatic period. Hence, the highly favorable conditions that allowed the greatest population growth ultimately led to catastrophic collapse once the climate deteriorated (Larson et al. 1996). Beginning about AD 1000, the Tavaputs Plateau climates became unusually wet, it became feasible to grow tremendous amounts of food to support a larger population, and indeed populations expanded into every niche where it was possible to grow maize. And then, just as suddenly, the climates

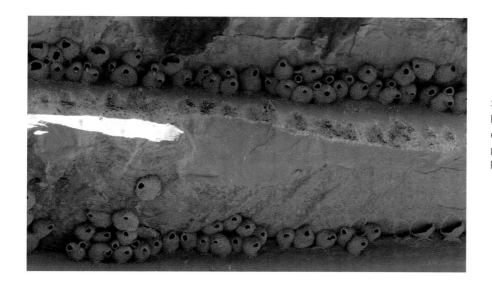

Swallows now reside where the Fremont people once carved, etched, scratched, pecked, and painted their images. Photo by Ray Boren.

reverted to more "normal" conditions—drier and less conducive to agriculture. The local environment could not support the larger population that had been lulled into a false sense of reality that "wet" was normal. And populations retracted.

As recent tree-ring studies have demonstrated (Knight et al. 2009), the twentieth century, when taken in the context of the past 1,800 years, is also among the wetter cycles recorded, although not as wet as a cycle in the AD 1300s or another in the early 1600s. It was punctuated by several severe short-term droughts, but it was a wet cycle nonetheless. And during the same hundred years, as western populations soared, the demands on limited water grew exponentially. It is quite possible that society today has also been lulled into a false sense of reality that "current" conditions are normal, when in fact 1,800 years of climatic history say otherwise, that there will be dramatically less water when climates return to drier historical norms. Three of the driest years on record—1934, 1977, and 2002—occurred during the recent abnormal wet cycle.

What will happen when similar extreme droughts descend on the West during a normal dry cycle? As the tree-ring scientists warn, "Such conditions could be stressful even for water-supply systems with considerable multi-year storage" (Knight et al. 2009:8). The rise and fall of the Fremont in Nine Mile Canyon could well be a cautionary lesson for all who live in the arid West.

References

Allison, James
2010 Julian Steward's Uintah River Mounds. Paper
presented at the annual meeting of the Great Basin
Anthropological Conference, Layton, Utah.
Alter, J. Cecil
1932 *Utah, the Storied Domain: A Documentary
History of Utah's Eventful Career.* American
Historical Society, Chicago.
Ambler, J. Richard
1969 The Temporal Span of the Fremont. *Southwestern
Lore* 34(4):107–116. Boulder, Colorado.
Arnold-Boomgarden, Shannon
2008 A Viewshed Analysis of Stored Resources in Range
Creek Canyon, Central Utah. Poster presented
at the 70th Annual Meeting of the Society for
American Archaeology, Salt Lake City.
2009 An Application of ARCGIS Viewshed
Analysis in Range Creek Canyon, Utah.
Utah Archaeology 22(1):15–30.
Barlow, K. Renee
2002 Predicting Maize Agriculture among the
Fremont: An Economic Comparison of
Farming and Foraging in the American
Southwest. *American Antiquity* 67(1):65–88.
2006 A Formal Model for Predicting Agriculture among
the Fremont. In *Behavioral Ecology and the Transition
to Agriculture*, edited by Douglas J. Kennett and Bruce
Winterhalder. University of California Press, Berkeley.
Barlow, K. Renee, Ronald H. Towner,
and Mathew W. Salzer
2008 Fremont Granaries of Range Creek: Defensive
Maize Storage on the Northern Colorado
Plateau. Manuscript on file with the lead
author, College of Eastern Utah, Price.
Beckwith, Frank
1931 Some Interesting Pictographs in Nine Mile Canyon,
Utah. *El Palacio* 31(14):216–222. Santa Fe, New Mexico.

1932 Serpent Petroglyph in Nine Mile Canyon. *El
Palacio* 33(15–16):147–149. Santa Fe, New Mexico.
Benson, Larry V., Michael S. Berry, Edward
A. Jolie, Jerry D. Spangler, David W.
Stahle, and Eugene M. Hattori
2007 Possible Impacts of Early 11th, Middle 12th and
Late 13th Century Droughts on Western Native
Americans and the Mississippian Cahokians.
Quaternary Science Reviews 26:336–350.
Berry, Michael S., and Claudia F. Berry
2003 An Archaeological Analysis of the Prehistoric
Fremont Culture for the Purpose of Assessing
Cultural Affiliation with the Ten Claimant Tribes.
Manuscript on file, Upper Colorado Regional
Office, Bureau of Reclamation, Salt Lake City.
Bishop, Francis Marion
1947 Captain Francis Marion Bishop's Journal. *Utah
Historical Quarterly* 15(1–4):154–253. Salt Lake City.
Board of Regents
1937 Minutes of the March 17, 1937, meeting,
accepting the resignation of John Gillin.
University of Utah Archives, Salt Lake City.
Bowers, William
1931 Field Journal of the 1931 Claflin-Emerson
Expedition. Original on file, Peabody Museum,
Harvard University, Cambridge, Massachusetts.
Bradley, George Y.
1947 George Y. Bradley's Journal. *Utah Historical
Quarterly* 25(1–4):29–72. Salt Lake City.
Brew, John O.
1931 Field Journal of the 1931 Claflin-Emerson
Expedition. Original on file, Peabody Museum,
Harvard University, Cambridge, Massachusetts.
1932 February 15 letter to Noel Morss explaining
various aspects of excavations at Rasmussen
Cave. Peabody Museum, Harvard
University, Cambridge, Massachusetts.

1982 Noel Morss, 1904–1981. *American Antiquity* 47(2):344–345.

Bureau of Land Management
2008 Nine Mile Canyon. http://www.blm.gov/ut/st/en/fo/vernal/recreation_/nine_mile_canyon.html.

Carlyle, Shawn W., Ryan L. Parr, M. Geoffrey Hayes, and Dennis H. O'Rourke
2000 Context of Maternal Lineages in the Greater Southwest. *American Journal of Physical Anthropology* 113:85–101.

Castleton, Kenneth B.
1984 *Petroglyphs and Pictographs of Utah, Volume One.* Utah Museum of Natural History, Salt Lake City.
1987 *Petroglyphs and Pictographs of Utah, Volume Two.* Utah Museum of Natural History, Salt Lake City.

Castleton, Kenneth B., and David B. Madsen
1981 The Distribution of Rock Art Elements and Styles in Utah. *Journal of California and Great Basin Anthropology* 3(2):163–175. Banning, California.

Cole, Sally J.
1990 *Legacy on Stone.* Johnson Books, Boulder, Colorado.

Creasman, Steven D.
1981 *Archaeological Investigations in the Canyon Pintado Historic District, Rio Blanco County, Colorado.* Reports of the Laboratory of Public Archaeology No. 34. Colorado State University, Fort Collins, Colorado.

Creasman, Steven D., and Linda J. Scott
1987 Texas Creek Overlook: Evidence for Late Fremont (Post AD 1200) Occupation in Northwest Colorado. *Southwestern Lore* 53(4):1–16. Boulder, Colorado.

Darrah, William C.
1951 *Powell of the Colorado.* Princeton University Press, Princeton, New Jersey.

Dellenbaugh, Frederick S.
1877 The Shinumos—A Pre-Historic People of the Rocky Mountain Region. *Bulletin of the Buffalo Society of Natural Sciences* 3(4):168–180. Buffalo, New York.
1908 *A Canyon Voyage: The Narrative of the Second Powell Expedition down the Green-Colorado River from Wyoming, and the Explorations on Land, in the Years 1871–1872.* Yale University Press, New Haven, Connecticut.

Dennison, James
1931 Field Journal of the 1931 Claflin-Emerson Expedition. Original on file, Peabody Museum, Harvard University, Cambridge, Massachusetts.

Dernbach, Lisa Sue
1992 Reconstruction of Upper Holocene Stream Processes and Paleoclimatic Patterns in Kane County, Utah. Master's thesis, California State University, Long Beach.

Ferguson, C. W., Jr.
1949 Additional Dates for Nine Mile Canyon, Northeastern Utah. *Tree-Ring Bulletin* 16(2). Tucson, Arizona.

Flaim, Francis R.
1961 Infant Carrying Crib and Infant Burial. Accession receiving report, College of Eastern Utah Prehistoric Museum, Catalog No. A-94. Price, Utah.

Flaim, Francis R., and Austen D. Warburton
1961 Additional Figurines from Rasmussen Cave. *Masterkey* 35(1):19–24. Los Angeles.

Forbes, Waldo
1931 Field Journal of the 1931 Claflin-Emerson Expedition. Original on file, Peabody Museum, Harvard University, Cambridge, Massachusetts.

Fowler, Don D., and John F. Matley
1978 *The Palmer Collection from Southwestern Utah, 1875.* Miscellaneous Paper No. 20, University of Utah Anthropological Papers No. 99. University of Utah Press, Salt Lake City.

Gaumer, Alfred Elliot
1937 Basketmaker Caves in Desolation Canyon, Green River, Utah. *Masterkey* 11(5):160–165. Los Angeles.
1939 A Fremont River Culture Cradle. *Masterkey* 13(4):139–140. Los Angeles.

Geary, Edward A.
1981 Nine Mile: Eastern Utah's Forgotten Road. *Utah Historical Quarterly* 49(1):42–55. Salt Lake City.

Geib, Phil R.
1996 Formative Cultures and Boundaries: Reconsideration of the Fremont and Anasazi. In *Glen Canyon Revisited*, by Phil R. Geib, pp. 98–114. University of Utah Anthropological Papers No. 119. University of Utah Press, Salt Lake City.

Gillin, John L.
1935 July 3 Western Union telegram to George Thomas, president of the University of Utah, indicating his encouragement to his son to move west. Document on file, University of Utah Archives, Salt Lake City.

Gillin, John L., and John P. Gillin
1948 *Cultural Sociology.* Macmillan, New York.

Gillin, John P.
1934a The Barama River Caribs of British Guiana. Unpublished Ph.D. dissertation, Harvard University, Cambridge, Massachusetts.
1934b John P. Gillin vitae and references. Peabody Museum, Harvard University, Cambridge, Massachusetts.

1935a June 7 Western Union telegram to the Department of Sociology and Anthropology at the University of Utah, inquiring about a teaching vacancy. University of Utah Archives, Salt Lake City.

1935b June 24 letter to George Thomas, president of the University of Utah, outlining his health problems and interest in coming to the university. University of Utah Archives, Salt Lake City.

1935c July 3 letter to George Thomas, president of the University of Utah, accepting a teaching position with certain conditions. University of Utah Archives, Salt Lake City.

1935d July 5 Western Union telegram to George Thomas, president of the University of Utah, advising of his release from a commitment to the University of Cincinnati. University of Utah Archives, Salt Lake City.

1935e September 18 letter to Julian H. Steward at the University of California, seeking advice on Utah research opportunities and cultural resource laws. University of Utah Archives, Salt Lake City.

1935f September 18 letter to Byron Cummings at the University of Arizona, seeking advice on cultural resource protection laws. University of Utah Archives, Salt Lake City.

1935g October 4 letter to George Thomas, president of the University of Utah, outlining a proposal for cultural resource protection regulations. University of Utah Archives, Salt Lake City.

1935h October 8 letter to George Thomas, president of the University of Utah, amending his earlier recommendations for cultural resource protection regulations. University of Utah Archives, Salt Lake City.

1935i December 11 letter to George Thomas, president of the University of Utah, seeking a leave of absence. University of Utah Archives, Salt Lake City.

1936a Field Notes of Nine Mile Canyon. Handwritten notes and sketches on file, Utah Museum of Natural History, Salt Lake City.

1936b Trip to St. George, April 23–25, 1936. Memorandum. University of Utah Archives, Salt Lake City.

1936c April 7 letter to Donald Scott, director of the Peabody Museum, discussing sites along the Virgin and Santa Clara Rivers. Peabody Museum, Harvard University, Cambridge, Massachusetts.

1936d April 29 letter to Donald Scott, director of the Peabody Museum, discussing research potential of Santa Clara River area. Peabody Museum, Harvard University, Cambridge, Massachusetts.

1936e August 12 letter to Donald Scott, director of the Peabody Museum, discussing the summer's excavations in Nine Mile Canyon. Peabody Museum, Harvard University, Cambridge, Massachusetts.

1937a January 29 letter to Donald Scott, director of the Peabody Museum, discussing the potential of sites in the Marysvale area and Henry Mountains. Peabody Museum, Harvard University, Cambridge, Massachusetts.

1937b April 2 letter to George Thomas, president of the University of Utah, discussing the budget for the joint University of Utah–Peabody Museum Expedition. University of Utah Archives, Salt Lake City.

1937c April 16 letter to Dr. Beeley discussing the Nine Mile Canyon monograph. University of Utah Archives, Salt Lake City.

1937d April 30 letter to George Thomas, president of the University of Utah, detailing plans and budget for a joint University of Utah–Peabody expedition to Marysvale and Ephraim. University of Utah Archives, Salt Lake City.

1938 *Archaeological Investigations in Nine Mile Canyon, Utah (During the Year 1936).* Bulletin of the University of Utah 28(11). Salt Lake City.

1941 *Archeological Investigations in Central Utah: Joint Expedition of the University of Utah and the Peabody Museum, Harvard University.* Papers of the Peabody Museum of American Archeology and Ethnology 17(2). Harvard University, Cambridge, Massachusetts.

Gowans, Fred R.

1985 *Rocky Mountain Rendezvous.* Peregrine Smith Books, Layton, Utah.

Gunnerson, James H.

1955 Archaeological Survey: Preliminary Report of 1954 Reconnaissance. Manuscript on file, Department of Anthropology, University of Utah, Salt Lake City.

1957 *An Archaeological Survey of the Fremont Area.* University of Utah Anthropological Papers No. 28. University of Utah Press, Salt Lake City.

1959 The Utah Statewide Archeological Survey: Its Background and First Ten Years. *Utah Archeology* 5(4):3–16. Salt Lake City.

1960 The Fremont Culture: Internal Dimensions and External Relationships. *American Antiquity* 25(3):373–380.

1962 Three Wooden Shovels from Nine Mile Canyon. In *Miscellaneous Collected Papers,* edited by David M. Pendergast, pp. 1–7. University of Utah Anthropological Papers No. 60. University of Utah Press, Salt Lake City.

1969 *The Fremont Culture: A Study in Culture Dynamics on the Northern Anasazi Frontier.* Papers of the Peabody Museum of Archaeology and Ethnology 59(2). Harvard University, Cambridge, Massachusetts.

Harvard University Library

1998 John Phillip Gillin (1907–1973) Papers. Peabody Museum Archives 997–998, Harvard University, Cambridge, Massachusetts.

Hayden, Brian

1998 Practical and Prestige Technologies: The Evolution of Material Systems. *Journal of Archaeological Method and Theory* 5:1–55.

Holmes, William H.

1886 Pottery of the Ancient Pueblos. In *Fourth Annual Report of the Bureau of Ethnology,* by J. W. Powell, pp. 265–360. Government Printing Office, Washington, D.C.

Hurst, Winston

1999 The Professors' Legacy: Some Historical Insights into Southeastern Utah's Pothunting Tradition. Manuscript on file with the author, Blanding, Utah.

Hurst, Winston, and Bruce D. Louthan

1979 *Survey of Rock Art in the Central Portion of Nine Mile Canyon, Eastern Utah.* Publications in Archaeology, New Series No. 4. Brigham Young University, Provo, Utah.

Janetski, Joel C.

1997 150 Years of Utah Archaeology. *Utah Historical Quarterly* 65(2):100–133. Salt Lake City.

Jennings, Jesse D.

1959 Introductory History. In *Glen Canyon Archeological Survey: Part I,* by Don D. Fowler et al., pp. 1–13. University of Utah Anthropological Papers No. 39, Glen Canyon Series No. 6. University of Utah Press, Salt Lake City.

Johnson, Clay, and Byron Loosle

2002 *Prehistoric Uinta Mountain Occupations.* Ashley National Forest Heritage Report 2-02/2002. United States Department of Agriculture, U.S. Forest Service, Intermountain Region, Ogden, Utah.

Jones, Stephen Vandiver

1948 Journal of Stephen Vandiver Jones. *Utah Historical Quarterly* 26–27(1–4):10–174. Salt Lake City.

Judd, Neil

1926 *Archeological Investigations North of the Rio Colorado.* Bureau of American Ethnology Bulletin No. 82. Smithsonian Institution, Washington, D.C.

1954 Byron Cummings, 1860–1954. *American Antiquity* 20:154–157.

Kapches, Mima

2003 Profile: Henry Montgomery, Ph.D. (1849–1919), Professor of Archaeologic Geology. *Journal of the Ontario Archaeological Society* 75:29–37.

Kelly, Charles

1933 Don Maguire—Pioneer. *Utah Motorist,* April.

Kerns, Virginia

2003 *Scenes from the High Desert: Julian Steward's Life and Theory.* University of Illinois Press, Urbana.

Kidder, Alfred V., II

1931 Field Journal of the 1931 Claflin-Emerson Expedition. Original on file, Peabody Museum, Harvard University, Cambridge, Massachusetts.

Knight, Troy A., David M. Meko, and Christopher Baisan

2009 A Bimillennial-Length Tree-Ring Reconstruction of Precipitation for the Tavaputs Plateau, Northeastern Utah. *Quaternary Research,* doi:10.1016/j.yqres.2009.08.002.

LaPoint, Halcyon, Howard M. Davidson, Steven D. Creasman, and Karen C. Schubert

1981 *Archaeological Inventory in the Canyon Pintado Historic District, Rio Blanco County, Colorado.* Reports of the Laboratory of Public Archaeology No. 53. Colorado State University, Fort Collins.

Larson, Daniel O., Hector Neff, Donald A. Graybill, Joel Michaelsen, and Elizabeth Ambros

1996 Risk, Climatic Variability, and the Study of Southwestern Prehistory: An Evolutionary Perspective. *American Antiquity* 61(2):217–241.

LeBlanc, Steven A.

1999 *Prehistoric Warfare in the American Southwest.* University of Utah Press, Salt Lake City.

Liestman, Terri L.

1985 *Site 42Un1103: A Rockshelter in Dinosaur National Monument, Utah.* Midwest Archeological Center Occasional Studies in Anthropology No. 13. Lincoln, Nebraska.

Madsen, David B., and David Rhode

1994 Introduction to *Across the West: Human Population Movement and the Expansion of the Numa,* edited by David B. Madsen and David Rhode, pp. 3–5. University of Utah Press, Salt Lake City.

Madsen, David B., and Steven R. Simms
1998 The Fremont Complex: A Behavioral Perspective. *Journal of World Prehistory* 12(3):255–336.

Maguire, Don
1894 Report of the Department of Ethnology, Utah World's Fair Commission. In *Utah at the World's Columbian Exposition*, by E. A. McDaniel. Salt Lake Lithographics Press, Salt Lake City.
1997 *Gila Monsters and Red-Eyed Rattlesnakes: Don Maguire's Arizona Trading Expeditions, 1876–1879*. Edited by Gary Topping. University of Utah Press, Salt Lake City.

Matheny, Ray T.
1993 The 1992 Carbon County Nine Mile Canyon Archaeological and Historical Properties Survey. Manuscript on file, College of Eastern Utah Prehistoric Museum, Price, Utah.
2005 Nine Mile Canyon Rock Art and Fremont Survival Strategies. Paper presented at the annual meeting of the Utah Rock Art Research Association, October.

Matheny, Ray T., and Patti Alhand
1991 BYU Field School in Nine Mile Canyon. Manuscript on file, Department of Anthropology, Brigham Young University, Provo.

Matheny, Ray T., and Deanne G. Matheny
1990 The Fall 1989 Carbon County Nine-Mile Canyon Survey. Manuscript on file, Division of State History, Salt Lake City.

Matheny, Ray T., Deanne G. Matheny, Pamela Miller, and Blaine Miller
2004 Hunting Strategies and Winter Economy of the Fremont as Revealed in the Rock Art of Nine Mile Canyon. In *New Dimensions in Rock Art*, edited by Ray T. Matheny, pp. 145–193. Museum of Peoples and Cultures Occasional Papers Series No. 9. Provo, Utah.

Matheny, Ray T., Pamela Miller, and Deanne G. Matheny
1991 The 1990 Carbon County Nine Mile Canyon Archaeological Survey. Manuscript on file, Division of State History, Salt Lake City.
1992 The 1991 Carbon County Nine Mile Canyon Archaeological Survey. Manuscript on file, Division of State History, Salt Lake City.

Matheny, Ray T., Thomas S. Smith, and Deanne G. Matheny
1997 Animal Ethology Reflected in the Rock Art of Nine Mile Canyon, Utah. *Journal of California and Great Basin Anthropology* 19(1):70–103.

McDaniels, E. A.
1894 *Utah at the World's Columbian Exposition*. Salt Lake Lithographics Press, Salt Lake City.

McVaugh, Rogers
1956 *Edward Palmer: Plant Explorer of the American West*. University of Oklahoma Press, Norman.

Miller, Pamela W., and Deanne G. Matheny
1990 A Volunteer Survey in Nine Mile Canyon. *Utah Archaeology* 3(1):122–133. Salt Lake City.

Miller, Susan G.
1993 Human Remains from Site 42Cb584: A Descriptive Report. Paper presented at the 1st Rocky Mountain Anthropological Conference, Jackson, Wyoming.

Montgomery, Henry
1894 Prehistoric Man in Utah. *The Archaeologist* 2(8):227–234; 2(10):298–306; 2(11):335–342. Waterloo, Indiana.
1903 Prehistoric Man in the United States and Canada. Unpublished Ph.D. dissertation, Illinois Wesleyan University, Bloomington.

Moorehead, Warren K.
1892 In Search of a Lost Race. *Illustrated American*, August 6.

Morgan, Dale L.
1955 The Diary of William H. Ashley. *Bulletin of the Missouri Historical Society* 11(2–3). St. Louis.
1964 *The West of William H. Ashley, 1822–1838*. Old West Publishing Company, Denver, Colorado.

Morss, Noel
1928a Brief Report of the Peabody Museum Expedition in Utah, 1928. Unpublished manuscript on file, Peabody Museum, Harvard University, Cambridge, Massachusetts.
1928b Summary Report of the Peabody Museum Expedition in Utah, 1928. Unpublished manuscript on file, Peabody Museum, Harvard University, Cambridge, Massachusetts.
1931a *The Ancient Culture of the Fremont River in Utah*. Peabody Museum of American Archaeology and Ethnology 12(3). Harvard University, Cambridge, Massachusetts.
1931b Notes on the Archaeology of the Kaibito and Rainbow Plateaus in Arizona. Papers of the Peabody Museum of Harvard University 12(2). Cambridge.
1932 February 21 letter to J. O. Brew discussing the rarity of ceramics in Nine Mile Canyon. Peabody Museum, Harvard University, Cambridge, Massachusetts.
1960 May 17 letter to Otis Marston discussing his 1927 work in northern Arizona and conflicts with

Byron Cummings. Peabody Museum, Harvard University, Cambridge, Massachusetts.

1980 May 27 letter to J. Eldon Dorman indicating he has never been an archaeologist. Peabody Museum, Harvard University, Cambridge, Massachusetts.

O'Neill, Helen

2009 Town's Love for Indian Artifacts Backfires. *Salt Lake Tribune*, October 3.

Palmer, Edward

1876 Exploration of a Mound in Utah. *American Naturalist* 10:410–414. Boston.

1878 Cave Dwellings in Utah. *Eleventh Annual Report of the Peabody Museum of Archaeology and Ethnology* 2(2):269–272. Harvard University, Cambridge, Massachusetts.

Patterson, Jody J.

2009 Data Recovery at a Fremont Habitation (42Dc769) in Nine Mile Canyon, Duchesne County, Utah. Manuscript on file, Montgomery Archaeological Consultants, Moab, Utah.

Patterson, Jody J., and Tom H. Flanigan

2010 Capacity, Distribution and Spatial Associations of Granaries in Nine Mile Canyon: A Historical Ecology Perspective on Arable Acreage and Mobility. Paper presented at the annual meeting of the Great Basin Anthropological Conference, Layton, Utah.

Pennington, Campbell W.

1963 *The Tarahumara of Mexico: Their Environment and Material Culture.* University of Utah Press, Salt Lake City.

Phillips, Ann

1993 Archaeological Expeditions into Southeastern Utah and Southwestern Colorado between 1888–1898 and the Dispersal of Collections. In *Anasazi Basketmaker*, edited by Victoria M. Atkins, pp. 103–120. Utah Bureau of Land Management Cultural Resource Series No. 24. Salt Lake City.

Powell, John Wesley

1879 *Report on the Lands of the Arid Region of the United States, with a More Detailed Account of the Lands in Utah.* 45th Congress, 2nd Session, H.R. Exec. Doc. 73. Government Printing Office, Washington, D.C.

1947 Major Powell's Journal. *Utah Historical Quarterly* 25(1–4):125–139. Salt Lake City.

1961 *Exploration of the Colorado River and Its Tributaries.* Dover Press, New York. Originally published in 1895 under the title *Canyons of the Colorado.*

Powell, Walter C.

1948 Journal of W. C. Powell. *Utah Historical Quarterly* 26–27(1–4):252–490. Salt Lake City.

Powers, Willow

1990 March 8 letter to H. Blaine Phillips regarding the availability of the Albert Reagan photograph collection at the Laboratory of Anthropology, Museum of New Mexico, Santa Fe. Original on file with Bureau of Land Management, Vernal, Utah.

Putnam, Frederick Ward

1879 The Pueblo Ruins and the Interior Tribes. In *United States Geographical Surveys West of the One Hundredth Meridian, Vol. VII—Archaeology*, pp. 315–390. Government Printing Office, Washington, D.C.

Reagan, Albert B.

1931a Additional Archaeological Notes on Ashley and Dry Fork Canyons in Northeastern Utah. *El Palacio* 31(8):122–131. Santa Fe, New Mexico.

1931b Ancient Agriculturists of Brush Creek Valley, in Northeastern Utah. *The Frontier* 12:174–176.

1931c Archaeological Notes on the Brush Creek Region, Northeastern Utah. *Wisconsin Archeologist* 10(4):132–138. Milwaukee.

1931d Collections of Ancient Artifacts from the Ashley–Dry Fork District of the Uintah Basin, with Some Notes on the Dwellings and Mortuary Customs of the Ouray Indians of the Ouray (Utah) Region. *El Palacio* 31(26):407–413. Santa Fe, New Mexico.

1931e Early House Builders of the Brush Creek Region in Northeastern Utah. *American Anthropologist* 33(4):660–661.

1931f Notes from the Field. *Discoveries* 2(2):8.

1931g Pictographs of Ashley and Dry Fork Valleys in Northeastern Utah. *Transactions of the Kansas Academy of Science* 34:168–216. Lawrence.

1931h Ruins and Pictographs in Nine Mile Canyon, Utah. *Transactions of the Illinois State Academy of Science* 24(2):369–370. Springfield.

1931i Some Archaeological Notes on Hill Canyon in Northeastern Utah. *El Palacio* 31(15):223–244. Santa Fe, New Mexico.

1931j Some Archaeological Notes on Nine Mile Canyon, Utah. *El Palacio* 31(4):45–71. Santa Fe, New Mexico.

1931k Some Notes on the Ancient Earth-Lodge Peoples of the Willard Stage of Pueblo Culture in the Uintah Basin, Utah. *El Palacio* 30(19–20):236–241. Santa Fe, New Mexico.

1932a Indian Pictures in Ashley and Dry Fork Valleys, in Northeastern Utah. *Art and Archaeology* 34(4):200–205, 210. Washington, D.C.

1932b Utah: Report of 1931 Field Season. *American Anthropologist* 34(3):505.

1933a Anciently Inhabited Caves of the Vernal (Utah) District, with Some Additional Notes on Nine Mile Canyon, Northeast Utah. *Transactions of the Kansas Academy of Science* 36:41–70. Lawrence.

1933b Caves of the Vernal District of Northeastern Utah. *Utah Academy of Sciences, Arts and Letters* 10:13–18. Salt Lake City.

1933c Evidence of Migration in Ancient Pueblo Times. *American Anthropologist* 35(1):206–207.

1933d Utah: Report of Investigations. *American Anthropologist* 35(3):508.

1933e Some Notes on the Snake Pictographs of Nine Mile Canyon, Utah. *American Anthropologist* 35(3):550–551.

1933f Summary of Archaeological Finds in the Uintah Basin, in Utah, to Date. *Utah Academy of Sciences, Arts and Letters* 10:3–9. Salt Lake City.

1934a Evidence of a Possible Migration in the Very Dawning Period of Pueblo Culture. *Primitive Man* 7(1):12–14. Washington, D.C.

1934b Some Ancient Indian Granaries. *Utah Academy of Sciences, Arts and Letters* 11:39–40. Salt Lake City.

1935a Archaeological Report of Field Work Done in Utah in 1934–35. *Utah Academy of Sciences, Arts and Letters* 12:50–88. Salt Lake City.

1935b Petroglyphs Show That the Ancients of the Southwest Wore Masks. *American Anthropologist* 37(3):707–708.

1935c Two Rock Pictures and Their Probable Connection with the "Pied Piper" Myth of the Indians. *Colorado Magazine* 12(2):55–59. Denver.

1937 Ancient Utah People Seem to Have Believed That Snakes Evolved from an Animal. *Wisconsin Archaeologist* 15(2):44. Milwaukee.

Reed, Lori Stephens, C. Dean Wilson, and Kelley A. Hays-Gilpin
2000 From Brown to Gray: The Origins of Ceramic Technology in the Northern Southwest. In *Foundations of Anasazi Culture: The Basketmaker-Pueblo Transition*, edited by Paul F. Reed, pp. 203–230. University of Utah Press, Salt Lake City.

Reina, Ruben E.
1976 Obituaries: John Phillip Gillin, 1907–1973. *American Anthropologist* 78:79–86.

Roberts, Henry
1928 Summary of the 1929 Field Season. Manuscript on file, Peabody Museum of Archaeology and Ethnology, Harvard University.

Robins, Michael R.
1997 Modeling Socioeconomic Organization of the San Juan Basketmakers: A Preliminary Study in Rock Art and Social Dynamics. In *Early Farmers of the Northern Southwest: Papers on Chronometry, Social Dynamics and Ecology*, edited by F. E. Smiley and M. R. Robins, pp. 73–120. Animas-LaPlata Archaeological Project Research Paper No. 7. Northern Arizona University, Flagstaff.

2002 Status and Social Power: Rock Art as Prestige Technology among the San Juan Basketmakers of Southeast Utah. In *Traditions, Transitions and Technologies: Themes in Southwestern Archaeology*, edited by Sarah H. Schlanger, pp. 386–400. University Press of Colorado, Boulder.

Robins, Michael R., and Kelley A. Hays-Gilpin
2000 The Bird in the Basket: Gender and Social Change in Basketmaker Iconography. In *Foundations of Anasazi Culture: The Basketmaker-Pueblo Transition*, edited by Paul F. Reed, pp. 231–247. University of Utah Press, Salt Lake City.

Rudy, Jack R.
1953 *An Archeological Survey of Western Utah*. University of Utah Anthropological Papers No. 12. University of Utah Press, Salt Lake City.

1954 University of Utah Archaeological Fieldwork, 1952–1953. *Southwestern Lore* 19(4):13–15. Boulder, Colorado.

1955 *Archaeological Excavations in Beef Basin, Utah*. University of Utah Anthropological Papers No. 20. University of Utah Press, Salt Lake City.

Rudy, Jack R., and Robert D. Stirland
1950 *An Archeological Reconnaissance in Washington County, Utah*. University of Utah Anthropological Papers No. 9. University of Utah Press, Salt Lake City.

Schaafsma, Polly
1970 Survey Report of the Rock Art of Utah. Manuscript on file, Antiquities Section, Division of State History, Salt Lake City.

1971 *The Rock Art of Utah: From the Donald Scott Collection*. Papers of the Peabody Museum 65. Harvard University, Cambridge, Massachusetts.

Schulman, Edmund
1948 Dendrochronology in Northeastern Utah. *Tree-Ring Bulletin* 15:2–14. Tucson, Arizona.

1950 A Dated Beam from Dinosaur National Monument. *Tree-Ring Bulletin* 16(3):18–19. Tucson, Arizona.

1951 Miscellaneous Ring Records. *Tree-Ring Bulletin* 17(4):28–30. Tucson, Arizona.

1954 Dendroclimatic Changes in Semiarid Regions. *Tree-Ring Bulletin* 20(3–4):26–40. Tucson, Arizona.

Scott, Donald

1929 December 21 letter to Noel Morss detailing efforts to publish the Fremont culture monograph. Peabody Museum, Harvard University, Cambridge, Massachusetts.

1930a November 15 letter inviting Noel Morss to participate in a gathering of scholars to address problems in southwestern archaeology. Peabody Museum, Harvard University, Cambridge, Massachusetts.

1930b December 18 letter to Noel Morss requesting payment for the Fremont culture monograph. Peabody Museum, Harvard University, Cambridge, Massachusetts.

1931a Field Notes of the Claflin-Emerson Expedition, 1931 Field Season. Manuscript on file, Peabody Museum, Harvard University, Cambridge, Massachusetts.

1931b January 9 letter acknowledging $500 payment from Noel Morss for the Fremont culture monograph. Peabody Museum, Harvard University, Cambridge, Massachusetts.

1931c May 18 letter acknowledging $1,250 payment from Noel Morss for the Fremont culture monograph, and a total of $1,850 received. Peabody Museum, Harvard University, Cambridge, Massachusetts.

1936a April 2 letter to John P. Gillin advising him to consider investigations in the St. George, Parowan, and Paragonah areas. Peabody Museum, Harvard University, Cambridge, Massachusetts.

1936b August 19 letter to John P. Gillin, discussing a joint University of Utah–Peabody Museum expedition. Peabody Museum, Harvard University, Cambridge, Massachusetts.

Shaffer, Karen A., and Neva Garner Greenwood

1988 *Maud Powell: Pioneer American Violinist.* Iowa State University Press, Ames.

Smiley, T. L.

1951 *A Summary of Tree-Ring Dates from Some Southwestern Archaeological Sites.* University of Arizona Laboratory Bulletin of Tree-Ring Research No. 5. Tucson.

Smith, Melvin T.

1987 Before Powell: Exploration of the Colorado River. *Utah Historical Quarterly* 55(2):105–119. Salt Lake City.

Spangler, Jerry D.

1993 Site Distribution and Settlement Patterns in Lower Nine Mile Canyon: The Brigham Young University Surveys of 1989–91. Master's thesis, Brigham Young University, Provo, Utah.

2000a One-Pot Pithouses and Fremont Paradoxes. In *Intermountain Archaeology*, edited by David Madsen and Michael Metcalf, pp. 25–38. University of Utah Anthropological Papers No. 122. University of Utah Press, Salt Lake City.

2000b Old Paradigms and New Perspectives: Radiocarbon Dates, Acquired Wisdom and the Search for Temporal Order in the Uinta Basin. In *Intermountain Archaeology*, edited by David Madsen and Michael Metcalf, pp. 48–68. University of Utah Anthropological Papers No. 122. University of Utah Press, Salt Lake City.

2002 Paradigms and Perspectives Revisited: A Class I Overview of Cultural Resources in the Uinta Basin and Tavaputs Plateau. Manuscript on file, Bureau of Land Management, Vernal, Utah.

2008 *Dust Up: A Baseline Site Condition Assessment and Analysis of Dust Accumulation and Vandalism in the Cottonwood Canyon Confluence Area, Nine Mile Canyon, Carbon County, Utah.* Colorado Plateau Archaeological Alliance, Ogden, Utah.

2009 *The Nutter Ranch Project: A Preliminary Report of the 2008 Intuitive Surveys.* Colorado Plateau Archaeological Alliance, Ogden, Utah.

2011a *Formal Site Documentation and Analysis of Visitor Impacts at Warrior Ridge (42Dc1), Duchesne County, Utah.* Colorado Plateau Archaeological Alliance, Ogden, Utah.

2011b *Of Owls and Cranes: A Cultural Resource Inventory of Section 35, Township 11 South Range 15 East, Duchesne County, Utah.* Colorado Plateau Archaeological Alliance, Ogden, Utah.

Spangler, Jerry D., James Aton, and Donna K. Spangler

2007 *Baseline Site Condition Assessment of Historic Properties near the Bureau of Land Management Ranger Station at Sand Wash, Uintah County.* Colorado Plateau Archaeological Alliance, Ogden, Utah.

Spangler, Jerry D., K. Renee Barlow, and Duncan Metcalfe

2004 *A Summary of the 2002–2003 Intuitive Surveys of the Wilcox Acquisition and Surrounding Lands, Range Creek Canyon.* Utah Museum of Natural History Occasional Papers. University of Utah, Salt Lake City.

Spangler, Jerry D., and Kevin T. Jones

2009 *Land of Wildest Desolation: Final Report of the Desolation Canyon Intuitive Surveys and Baseline Site Condition Assessments of 2006 to 2008.* Colorado Plateau Archaeological Alliance, Ogden, Utah.

Spangler, Jerry D., Andrew T. Yentsch, Joel
   Boomgarden, and Shannon Arnold
2006 *Data Recovery at Two High Elevation
   Archaic Residential Base Camps (42Cb2178 and
   42Cb2186) and a Historic Homestead (432Cb2185),
   on the West Tavaputs Plateau, Carbon County,
   Utah*. Colorado Plateau Archaeological
   Alliance, Ogden, Utah.

Steward, John F.
1948 Journal of John F. Steward. *Utah Historical
   Quarterly* 26–27(1–4):174–251. Salt Lake City.

Steward, Julian H.
1929a The Ceremonial Buffoon of the American
   Indian: A Study of Ritualized Clowning and
   Role Reversals. Unpublished Ph.D. dissertation,
   University of California, Berkeley.
1929b *Petroglyphs of California and Adjoining States*.
   University of California Publications in American
   Archaeology and Ethnology No. 24. Berkeley.
1933 Early Inhabitants of Western Utah: Part I. *Bulletin
   of the University of Utah* 23(7):1–34. Salt Lake City.
1940 Native Cultures of the Intermontane (Great
   Basin) Area. *Smithsonian Miscellaneous
   Collections* 100:445–502. Washington, D.C.

Strevell, C. N., and C. S. Pulver
1935 Report of the Utah State Museum Association
   Archaeological Expedition. Manuscript on file,
   Utah Division of State History, Salt Lake City.

Sumner, John C.
1947 J. C. Sumner's Journal. *Utah Historical
   Quarterly* 25(1–4):108–124. Salt Lake City.

Sun Advocate
1970 Minnie and Maud—Canyons Named after
   Twin Girls. *Sun Advocate*, November 5.

Swanson, Frederick H.
2007 *Dave Rust: A Life in the Canyons*. University
   of Utah Press, Salt Lake City.

Talbot, Richard K.
2000 Fremont Architecture. In *Clear Creek
   Canyon Archaeological Project: Results and
   Synthesis*, pp. 131–184. Museum of Peoples
   and Cultures Occasional Papers No. 7.
   Brigham Young University, Provo, Utah.

Talbot, Richard K., and Lane D. Richens
1996 *Steinaker Gap: An Early Fremont Agriculture
   Farmstead*. Museum of Peoples and Cultures
   Technical Series No. 94-18. Brigham
   Young University, Provo, Utah.

Tanner, Vasco M.
1939 Albert B. Reagan, 1871–1936. *Utah Academy
   of Sciences* 16:5–19. Salt Lake City.

Thomas, George
1935a June 27 letter to John Gillin, praising the
   University of Utah as ideal for Gillin's
   convalescence. University of Utah
   Archives, Salt Lake City.
1935b June 27 letter to John L. Gillin, enlisting his
   support in the recruitment of his son, John P.
   Gillin, to the University of Utah. University
   of Utah Archives, Salt Lake City.
1935c June 27 letter to Herman Schneider, president
   of the University of Cincinnati, seeking John
   Gillin's release from a teaching commitment there.
   University of Utah Archives, Salt Lake City.
1935d July 9 Western Union telegram to John P. Gillin,
   confirming his appointment to the university.
   University of Utah Archives, Salt Lake City.
1935e December 14 letter to John P. Gillin
   granting a leave of absence. University
   of Utah Archives, Salt Lake City.
1937 March 20 letter to John P. Gillin,
   accepting Gillin's resignation. University
   of Utah Archives, Salt Lake City.

Thompson, Almon Harris
1939 Diary of Almon Harris Thompson, edited
   by Herbert E. Gregory. *Utah Historical
   Quarterly* 7(1–3):2–140. Salt Lake City.

Thompson, Patricia J.
1993 Excavations in Nine Mile Canyon from 1892–
   1990: A Study in Cultural Diversity. Master's
   thesis, Brigham Young University, Provo, Utah.

Trigger, Bruce G.
1989 *A History of Archaeological Thought*. Cambridge
   University Press, Cambridge.

Turner, Christy G., II, and Jacqueline A. Turner
1999 *Man Corn: Cannibalism and Violence in the
   Prehistoric American Southwest*. University
   of Utah Press, Salt Lake City.

Tyler, S. Lyman
1951 Before Escalante: An Early History of the
   Yuta Indians of the Area North of New
   Mexico. Unpublished Ph.D. dissertation,
   University of Utah, Salt Lake City.

University of Utah
1937 John P. Gillin: Historical Record of Members of
   the Faculty, with an attached vitae of degrees,

teaching assignments, and publications. University of Utah Archives, Salt Lake City.

Utah Parks Board
1935 Park Board Regulations for Enforcement of Utah Archaeology Law (Utah Revised Statutes 1933, Chapter 14). University of Utah Archives, Salt Lake City.

Van Cott, John W.
1990 *Utah Place Names: A Comprehensive Guide to the Origins of Geographic Names.* University of Utah Press, Salt Lake City.

Vander Wall, Stephen B.
1990 *Food Hoarding in Animals.* University of Chicago Press, Chicago.

Warner, Ted J. (editor)
1976 *The Domínguez–Escalante Journal: Their Expedition through Colorado, Utah, Arizona, and New Mexico in 1776.* Translated by Fray Angelico Chavez. Brigham Young University Press, Provo, Utah.

Wenger, Gilbert Riley
1956 An Archaeological Survey of Southern Blue Mountain and Douglas Creek in Northwestern Colorado. Master's thesis, University of Denver, Denver, Colorado.

Wheeler, George M.
1889 *Report upon United States Geographical Surveys West of the One Hundredth Meridian Vol. I—Geographical Report.* Government Printing Office, Washington, D.C.

Whitfield, A., J. Patterson, and J. Fritz
2006 West Tavaputs Plateau EIS Class I Cultural Resource Literature Review. Manuscript on file, Montgomery Archaeological Consultants, Moab, Utah.

Willey, Gordon R.
1988 *Portraits in American Archaeology.* University of New Mexico Press, Albuquerque.

Willey, Gordon R., and Jeremy A. Sabloff
1980 *A History of American Archaeology.* W. H. Freeman, New York.

Worster, Donald
2001 *A River Running West: The Life of John Wesley Powell.* Oxford University Press, New York.

Index

Numbers in italics refer to illustrations.

Neff, Hector, 174
Nephi, Utah, 29, 94, 95, 111
Nevills, Norman, 95
New York Philharmonic Society, 13
New York University, 87
Nine Mile Canyon: Albert Reagan's investigations in,
    73–79; Alfred Gaumer in, 64–69; Brigham Young
    University excavations in, 134–36; Brigham Young
    University surveys of, 136–43; Byron Cummings in,
    34; Castle Valley USAS surveys of, 131–34; Claflin-
    Emerson Expedition to, 54–58; Don Maguire in,
    28; effects of regional droughts on, 153–55, 174–75;
    environmental context, 1–2; Frank Beckwith in, 62;
    Henry Montgomery investigations in, 30–33; James
    Gunnerson's investigations in, 118–19; John Gillin
    investigations in, 96–107; John Steward's observations
    near, 21–22; Julian Steward's collections from, 42;
    lack of pottery in, 56, 149–52; looting of Rasmussen
    Cave, 62–69; Minnie Maud Creek, 11–14; mobile
    farmers in, 156–58; name origins, 2, 3; Noel Morss
    investigations in, 49–50; Public Archaeology Research
    Group inventory in, 129–31; Ray T. Matheny's rock
    art studies, 127–29; related to J. W. Powell expedition,
    3–11; rock art styles defined for, 121–24; Tavaputs
    adaptation, 146–51, 154–55, 161; temporal context for,
    165–69; tree-ring samples from, 108–10, 148, 154, 155;
    University of Santa Clara investigations in, 120–
    21; Utah Museum Association expedition to, 81–82
Nine Mile Creek, 1–3, 5–12, 10, 14, 15, 21, 52, 65, 68,
    109; A. H. Thompson's water flow tests of, 12
nine-mile triangulation, 3, 7
Nine Mile Valley, 14
Noe, E. S., 64; looting of Rasmussen Cave, 62–69
Nordell's Fort, 54, 54, 119, 119, 136
"Northern Periphery," 39
Nutter, Preston, 52
Nutter Ranch, 49, 52, 75, 76, 110, 166
Nyswander, Dorothy, 43

Ogden, Utah, 26, 27, 39
Ohio Historical Society, 25
Ohio State University, 112, 113
Olger Ranch Ruin, 110
Ontario, Canada, 29
On the Origin of Species (Darwin), 20
Ouray, Utah, 20, 69, 70
Owl Panel, 16, 17, 73, 118

Pace Ranch, 52–54, 134, 136
Paiute peoples, 41, 86; Shivwits Reservation, 96
El Palacio (journal), 62, 63
Paleoindians, 166
Palmer, Edward, 22–25
Paragonah, Utah, 24, 27–29, 95; excavations of mounds
    at, 28. See also Royal Palace of Paragonah
Patterson, Jody J., 157–58, 162, 164
Payson, Utah, 24, 27
Peabody Museum of Archaeology and Ethnology
    (Harvard University), vii, 22–25, 35, 39, 44, 44–49,
    45, 51, 56, 58, 62, 73, 85, 89, 91, 112, 113, 121, 122, 150
Pete's Canyon, 32
Pete's Village, 47, 119, 119
Peter's Point, 59
Piute County, Utah, 29
Phillips, Ann, 26, 33
Pig Rock, 74
Plain City, Utah, 27
playpens (prehistoric structures), 138
Poncho House, 95
pottery: black-on-white, 68, 152; general, 137; grayware,
    68, 74, 77, 100, 104, 107, 118, 149–53, 151; polychrome,
    78, 152; rarity of in Nine Mile Canyon, 56, 147,
    149–53; unspecified painted, 30; whole jars, 77
Powell, John Wesley, x, 1–3, 3, 9, 9–15, 11, 14, 17, 20,
    22; Colorado River Exploring Expedition,
    2–5, 3, 9, 10, 9–11, 14, 17, 21, 22; prominence
    in Washington, D.C., 14, 22; Report on the
    Lands of the Arid Region, 5, 11, 12, 14
Powell, Maud, 13–15, 14
Powell, Walter Clement, 9
Powell, William Bramwell, 13–14
Praying Goats panel, 75, 75
Pressett, Humbert, 120
Price, Utah, 1, 18, 121, 131
Price River, 5, 11
Promontory Point (cave site), 95
Provo, Utah, 27, 72
Public Archaeology Research Group, 129–31
Puebloan peoples, 20, 79, 95; Ancestral Puebloans,
    xi, 37, 38, 42, 72, 77, 78, 81, 86, 95, 110, 127, 149–50,
    152; Early Pueblo, 42, 51; Hopi, 78, 79; pre-Pueblo
    art, 65; Pueblo II period, 77, 80, 81, 147–49, 167
Pulver, C. S., 82
Putnam, Frederic, 22–23, 25–26

rabbit-skin blanket, 101

Stewart, John, 96
stone cairns (prehistoric), *138*
Streville, Mr., 27
Sumner, Jack, 7, 10
Sumner's Amphitheatre, 5, *5*, 7, *7*, 8, 10–12
Sunnyside, Utah, 109
Sunstone Village, 142
Surprise Rapid, 9
Talmage, James E., 33
Tarahumara, 156–57, 162
"Tavaputs adaptation," 146–51, 154–55, 161
Tavaputs Plateau, 44, 51, 117, 119, 122, 146, 149–54, 164, 165, 168, 169, 174; East Tavaputs Plateau, 4, *52*, 52, *53*, 109; West Tavaputs Plateau, 1, 4, 5, *6*, 56–58, 67, 111, 149, 157
Tehuas, 17, 20
Thomas, George, ix, 88–91, *89*, 112
Thompson, Almon Harris, 1, 9, *9*, 12
Thorne, Leo, *71*, 71, 73, 75
Three Canyon, 53
Tihuas, 20
Tooele, Utah, ix, 112
Tooele County, Utah, 29
Trail Canyon, 1, 53, 165
trapezoidal anthropomorphs (Fremont rock art), *23*, *66*, *82*, 122–24, *123*, *125*, *148*, *150*, *153*, *168*, *174*
tree-ring dates and dating, 85–86, 108–10, *141*, 148, 154–55
turkeys, 51, 74, 78, 82

Uinta Basin, 1, 41, 42, 44, 45, 51, 70, 71, 76, 77, 82, 115, 124, 147, 148, 151
Uinta River, 5, 7, 11, 42, 71
Uintah County, Utah, 52
Uintah County Regional History Center, 70, *71*
United States Army, 1
United States Forest Service, 117
United States Geological Survey, 14
United States Indian Field Service, 61, 69–70
University of Arizona, 40, 47, 108, 154
University of Berlin, 87
University of California, Berkeley, 35, 37
University of Cincinnati, 88–89
University of Michigan, 41
University of North Carolina, 113
University of North Dakota, 29
University of Pennsylvania, 35
University of Pittsburgh, *86*, 113
University of Santa Clara, 120
University of Toronto, 29, 33

University of Utah, ix, 28, 33, 37, 39–41, 43–44, 71, 72, 81, 83, 85–89, 91, 93, 97, 101, 110, 112–13, 115–16, 119, 121, 161; Archaeological and History Museum, 39; Archaeology Department, 39, 40; Department of Sociology and Anthropology, ix, 88, 89; Museum of Deseret University, 29; Marriott Library (Special Collections), 83; Museum of Anthropology, 116; School of Arts and Sciences, 39; University of Deseret, 28, 29; University of Utah Museum, xi, 91, 92, 112
University of Wisconsin, 86–87
Upper Colorado River Basin Salvage Program, 117
Upper Sky House, 100, 110
Utah Avocational Archaeologist Certification Program, 132
Utah County, Utah, 29
Utah Division of State History, *163*
Utah Emergency Relief Administration, 82
Utah Historical Quarterly, *15*
Utah Museum Association, 81, 82; expedition, 82–83
Utah Museum of Natural History, 116, 126
Utah State Historical Society, *3*, *26*, *39*, *41*, 83
Utah State Parks Board, 81, 90, 92
Utah State Parks Commission, 117
Utah State Planning Board, 82
Utah State Road Commission, 82, 117
Utah Statewide Archaeological Society (USAS), 131–32, 142; Castle Valley Chapter, 131–32
Utah Statewide Archeological Survey, 116–17
Utah Territorial World's Fair Commission, 26–28, 32
Ute peoples, 22, 34, 35, 41, 70, 86; Ancestral Utes, 80, 81, 141; Ancestral Ute basket, *141*, 141; reservation, 49; Sun Dance, 41; Uinta Agency, 10, 21; Uinta Utes, 35

Valley Village, ix, 85, 96–100, *98*, *99*, 108, 115, 132, 145; House B at, 97–99; House C at, 99–100
Van Cott, John W., 3
Vernal, Utah, 73, 75, 80, 123, 126
Victoria University, 29
Virgin City, Utah, 117
Virgin River, 27

Warburton, Austen D., 120–21
Warrior Ridge, *84*; rock art, *87*, *88*, *90*, *91*, *93*, *96*, 97, *103*, 103–7, *105*, *106*, *107*, *111*, 172–73
Washington City, Utah, 24, 96
Water Canyon, 157
Waterpocket Fold, 44, *49*, 49
Wheeler, George, 20, 22, 27
White Canyon, 39